THE CORRIDOR OF LIGHT

Day of the Deathmongers

Rob Scarborough

RJS Publishing

CONTENTS

The Corridor Of Light
By Rob Scarborough

INTRODUCTION

Warning: This book contains graphic
descriptions of death and destruction.

<u>The deadly animal, killer charts:</u>

Many animals on earth are responsible for
human fatalities. Snakes kill fifty thousand people
every year, dogs twenty five thousand (including
through rabies), crocodiles, one thousand, and
lions one hundred.

But there are bigger (or should I say smaller)
surprises at the top of the death charts.

Tapeworms and Roundworms cause four
thousand five hundred fatalities, and freshwater
snails increase the toll by a hundred thousand per
annum. But the deadliest killer is a tiny insect.

Have you guessed? Yes, the mosquito leaves about
one million humans dead per annum; that's about
twice as many people as people kill.

As for wasps and hornets, fatal attacks number
only a few hundred each season, so what is
it that makes most of us hate and fear THEM
so much? Maybe it's the sight of that bulging
tiger-striped abdomen, needlepoint sting and the
incessant buzzing which accompanies imminent
attack? Or is it the thought of the wasp venom

teaming through our veins to trigger a painful and lingering reaction?

The two-inch long (five cm), Asian Giant Hornet has a poison-packed stinger, capable of dissolving human flesh to leave a hole the size of a bullet wound. Then there's the fierce Tarantula Hawk; the world's biggest wasp. This lethal critter risks death by dual as it tries to inject eggs into the Tarantula spider's abdomen. If successful, hundreds of deadly wasp larvae hatch, devouring the living Tarantula from the inside out and probably doing mankind a big favour at the same time.

Evidence of a good side to wasps is provided by at least two important facts. Worker wasps are amazing plant pollinators and also feed around five thousand pests, such as aphids and beetle larvae, to their young every year. This helps plants flourish in accordance with nature, and shows that we should perhaps treat wasps respectfully and as one of man's best friends.

Overall, the members of the order, Apocrita, which includes wasps and hornets, are a mixed bunch. Some have nasty traits and are not to be trusted, but other wasps are helpful to mankind, which brings me to my story.

*The year is 1979, on a
Lincolnshire farm:*

CHAPTER 1. MISSING PRESUMED DEAD

A wasp dropped in through the open sunroof and bounced slowly across the car windscreen before turning to hover, inches from Harry's nose. The young inventor froze. He was fixated by two jagged mandibles clicking together menacingly, while a pair of slender antennae twitched as the evil predator analysed the scene.

The tiny wasp was not in the least bit scared of Harry, but Harry was extremely scared of the tiny wasp. In particular, he was petrified by the insect's throbbing tiger-striped abdomen, needlepoint sting and dangling black legs, poised to grip his skin while the venom pumped into him. Harry gulped, but he dared not blink. Beads of sweat poured from his forehead, dripped over is eyebrows and ran down both cheeks as he focused on two large compound eyes and three smaller ones in between, all of which were drilling into him with malicious intent. After remaining still for as long as his nerves would allow, two seconds later, he flung open the car door and dived out.

Getting up from the dirt, Harry dusted off his flared jeans and wriggled both shoulders uncomfortably.

"What's up?" asked Lou. "Did you accidentally look in the car mirror and see yourself? cuz that would be enough to make anyone take fright."

"No. A wasp nearly stung me," spluttered Harry. "It was right there, hovering at the end of my nose and I'm sure wasps are getting bigger these days. I've heard that GIANT Asian hornets are about to spread throughout this country. What will we do then?" His face took on a look of acute alarm at the mere thought, while Lou joined in fervently on the subject.

"Too right. Hornet venom is powerful stuff. Their sting melts through human flesh, leaving a hole the size of a bullet wound. And then there's the anaphylactic shock. You'd be a gonner for sure if you upset a giant hornet or its nest!"

At that moment, Lou squealed and jabbed a finger into the air above her brother.

"Lookout, another wasp!!"

The shrill warning sent Harry into a full spin. With helicopter hands twirling above his head, he made a frantic attempt to fend off any new wasp attack, but moments later the sound of jeering confirmed he'd been tricked.

"You big baby. Petrified of an itsy bitsy wasp, are you?" Lou loved nothing more than teasing her little brother, a desire stemming from Harry's sudden adoption into HER family, six years earlier. In that single moment Lou saw herself demoted from only child to second favourite and belittling Harry was now a weapon of choice, which she wielded viciously whenever possible.

Gathering himself after the wasp incident, Harry cautiously re-entered the car, feeling more relaxed. He dropped into the driver's seat, grabbed the steering wheel and savoured the warm rays of sunshine that streamed down through his newly created sunroof. Peering out through the front windscreen, Harry pondered his latest modifications. Twin spotlights, mounted inside old five-litre paint tins had been riveted to a freshly painted, lime green bonnet and the jutting lamps reminded him of the bulging eyes of a frog. Tapping the dashboard three times he addressed the car. "I hereby name you Rivet," he said in a pleased with himself voice, before slumping back against the vinyl seat to dream of the adventures made possible by his latest alterations.

Harry's car, bought on the occasion of his thirteenth birthday as a field runabout, had been paid for with reward money earned after he and

Lou rounded up a pair of jewel thieves found hiding on their farm two years earlier.

The desire to re-design his car came from Harry's adoption into the Scrambles' family, aged six. Ever since then, he had invested maximum effort into emulating his new father, John Scrambles, an inventor with several successful farm gadgets under his belt. Harry's ideas, however, usually ended in disaster, much to the delight of his spiteful tomboy sister, on hand to offer false encouragement, before teasing him over the catastrophic results.

With Harry's latest automobile innovations catching Lou's attention across the stackyard, she broke off from polishing her trail bike.

"Scourgeeo, you steaming reprobate, where've your car's front wings gone? And what's with those oversized baked bean cans strapped to the bonnet?"

"The wings were rusty and full of holes so I ripped them completely off," replied Harry. And the paint tins contain spotlights, but what do you think to my new sunroof? Cool, eh?" He waved an arm through the gaping hole above his head and nodded in agreement with himself, expecting a positive reaction. Instead, Lou shook her head slowly from side to side.

Very cool, yes I agree! And wet when it rains; you pleb." She turned her head in disgust and went back to polishing the motorbike.

Later, at lunchtime, Lou mentioned Rivet again, this time in a more friendly tone of voice.

"Have you finished pratting about with that car yet, Harry? Cuz I wanna go out in it. I fancy being like the Pope in his Pope-mobile. You know? Standing up through the sunroof to wave at my followers." She grinned across the table as Harry slapped a beefburger on a piece of toast, added a large dollop of tomato sauce, then squeezed another round on top, taking a large bite from the dripping sandwich before answering.

"All done and dusted. I even got my inverter wired in, ready for fitting a turbocharger," he confirmed between munches. "We'll take Rivet for a test drive along the Green Lane if you like. I fancy exploring those abandoned air-raid shelters up by the airfield." He wiped sauce from the corner of his mouth onto the back of one hand, licking it off while throwing a sideways glance at his father, John Scrambles, whose head had suddenly popped up above the newspaper.

"You two should keep away from those old bunkers, they're not safe, and I don't mean structurally, either."

"Well, what do you mean, Dad?" asked both siblings, simultaneously. John Scrambles turned his head slowly and gazed out of the window before answering with a hint of sadness.

"The air raid shelters mark the spot your Grandpa Bert went missing, thirty-six years ago. And he's never been seen since."

This shocking remark sent Lou and Harry into an unusual state of silence. They had seldom heard their father talk about his own father's disappearance before, always assuming that Bert going missing was a normal consequence of the war. But now there seemed to be a more sinister twist, and the siblings' level of interest rose significantly.

Harry shoved the last of the toast roughly into his mouth and watched his father cross the room to the sideboard where he rummaged in a drawer for several seconds, then pulled out a black and white photograph. "Hah," exclaimed John, offering the picture to Harry.

"Your Grandpa Bert always chewed on a stalk of grass while walking around the farm checking his crops. I took this photo the day he disappeared; here, look."

After rubbing leftover red sauce from his fingertips onto the tablecloth, Harry gripped the photo in one hand and held it up in the light.

"Wow! So that's Grandpa Bert. What do you think happened, then? I mean, he couldn't have just vanished into thin air, could he?"

"But that's just it, though. Your Grandpa did just vanish. One minute we were clearing a site for the

Air Ministry to build three new air-raid shelters, the next, he was gone. Obliterated in a bomb blast according to Military Police, but I'm not so sure." A look of deep anguish fell across John's face giving away the haunting doubt that had plagued him for thirty-six years. Then, after pausing briefly, he moved on in a more matter-of-a-fact way.

"I was your age at the time, younger in fact. Mum took over the farm, with me helping at weekends. Times were hard. It was the middle of the war. Times were very hard."

Upon listening to these words, Harry was suddenly overcome with a desperation to relieve his father's angst, but equally, the prospect of a new mystery to crack, excited him to his very bones. Solving the conundrum of Grandpa Bert's disappearance would surely cement his rightful place in the Scrambles family. Even Lou might be impressed, he thought as John continued.

"Well, anyway. You've heard my warning. I say avoid the entire area. Those air-raid shelters are bad news."

Harry studied the strained look on his father's face and realising that now was not the best time to pursue the matter, shook his head in Lou's direction, but she was having none of it.

"Don't worry, Dad, we'll be super wary up at the bunkers and be back in time for tea, I promise," she said.

Their father grumbled something under his breath and reached for his cap with a frown. "Well, if you do go anywhere near those old buildings, remember what I've said. Be careful. Be very careful."

Moving the conversation on quickly, Harry related the wasp in the car story and was surprised when, after listening carefully, the siblings' father brought up an important point.

"Wasps may seem like a hideous waste of space, but remember this. Every living creature has a purpose in the world, not just the gentle things."

Harry paused to consider his father's words before launching a counter-argument.

"That's all very well, Dad, but wasp and hornet stings kill more people every year than bears OR sharks do? They've a lot of making up to do for that in my book."

The room fell into silent contemplation as the terrifying image of a giant hornet attack was lodged inside all of their heads.

CHAPTER 2. THE STANDING STONES

After lunch, Lou nipped away to feed her horse. She was looking forward to this new adventure with Harry. It would serve up plenty of opportunities to ridicule him.

As the horse approached, she shook half a bale of hay into a net at the edge of the paddock and stroked its mane, whispering in one ear. "Hey Dandy, how you doing? We'll go for a long ride later, I promise, but I've got some exploring to do with Harry, first." Lou patted the horse's neck and wandered back to the stackyard where Harry sat waiting in the car, eager to get going.

With the battered, lime-green Ford Anglia cruising up the lane, Lou pushed her way up through the hole in the roof.

"I'm queen," she shrieked, cascading her arms on either side in a right royal manner.

Minutes later, they parked by a bale stack at the side of the Green Lane and ventured into a wooded copse, tracking towards the abandoned air-raid shelters. Bantering as they went, Lou kicked things off. "Don't tell Dad, but I've already visited these shelters. The end bunker's been flattened, but I explored the other two. They were damp and spooky with writing scrawled all over the concrete walls. I suppose people in the war spent hours down there with nothing to do but add to the graffiti by candlelight." Harry nodded, confirming that he too had visited the site previously.

"When I came, there was a shimmering mirage hanging over the rubble of the demolished one, giving off a weird magnetic hum. Felt sort of like a paranormal forcefield. Proper eerie. I noticed a strange smell, too. Flowers, manure, and petrol, all mixed together, but only on that one spot. A few yards away everything was normal."

"Magnetic hum? Paranormal force field? Don't you mean vacuous hum and subnormal force field. Of the sort that usually emanate from your head, hah."

Harry replied to his sister indignantly. "You may laugh, but since Dad told us about Grandpa's disappearance, what I saw has taken on a whole new meaning. Dad was right; there's a dangerous feel to the whole area."

Suddenly, Harry stopped talking, raised a finger to his lips, and snatched Lou's arm. "Sshhh, I hear voices."

They ducked down and snuck towards a grassy

hillock with a set of steps leading into the dark war bunker. At the opposite end, a brick built chimney billowed out a mixture of white smoke and human voices, while slung on the ground nearby were two bicycles and a pair of backpacks. Cooking utensils tied by string, hung from the buckles of both bags.

As the siblings crept up the bank towards the chimney, the smell of burning wood filled their nostrils and the sound of familiar voices left them wide-eyed with disbelief. The gruff and nasal tones were unmistakably those of Stan and Bill, the Ginger Cake Gang. These were the villains who two years earlier, stole the queen's ruby from the Imperial State Crown, then holed up in derelict cottages on the edge of the Scrambles' farm. Harry and Lou had helped catch the crooks, earning a substantial reward with which each bought their own motor vehicle, Lou chose a trailbike, while Harry opted for an old car to run around the fields in.

But what were the thieves doing here, now? wondered Harry, cupping one hand over his ear and tuning into their conversation.

"That foolish Sergeant Grinly played right into our hands when he released us early with the map. He must know we need that piece of paper to find the ruby and he expects us to lead him to the burial site, but if he thinks that, he's got another think coming." Stan's trademark nasal laugh echoed up the chimney, followed by a haughty grunt as Bill responded in a gruff voice.

"But, how can we dig up the ruby and get away with it, though? If we go anywhere near Felton Hall, the police will start shadowing us. They know the missing gemstone is buried somewhere near there."

A burst of sparks flew from the chimney as Stan poked the fire aggressively before replying. "Don't you see, Bill? There's no need for us to dig up anything here and now. Instead, we'll crank up the Corridor of Light and travel in time to 2079. There, the ruby will have been missing for one hundred years. We can dig it up safely in the future AND tap into a massive reward, while seeming like the heroes of the day. Meanwhile, Sergeant Grinly, stuck here in 1979, will have no clue what's gone on. As far as he's concerned, we'll have vanished into thin air. It's the perfect plan."

Outside on the bank, Lou turned to Harry, furnishing a look of utter bewilderment. "Corridor of Light? 2079? What's he on about?" Harry stroked his chin thoughtfully without answering as Stan continued his conversation with Bill.

"The biggest problem we have is that the portal won't work until all of the stones are resurrected, and they are just laying in the grass at the moment. Even then, there will be one stone missing, so we'll need to lift up the five remaining stones and grab the girl's motorbike.

Her machine's the only thing fast enough to reactivate a weakened Corridor of Light now that our hoverboard is broken. She's always parking it with the keys left in. We'll follow her and wait for our chance to pinch it."

Stan cackled loudly, and his voice took on a self-congratulatory tone. "Just think, the very thieves who did the thieving, about to become heroes in a future world. We'll be untouchable by the laws of today and rich beyond our wildest dreams, what a beautiful irony. My idea is sheer brilliance, even if I do say so myself."

"Well, yes Stan. Apart from one fact. We've already been in prison for most of the time since arriving here through the time portal."

"Alright, alright," Snapped Stan, "But that's mainly on account of those darned interfering kids. Our sacrifice'll be worth it once we're famous and free in 2079. Just remember, with fame comes fortune. You mark my words; more money will be coming our way than we'd have ever have made selling the ruby on the black market. Picture us, starring in our own documentary, streamed to millions across multi-media channels worldwide as we unearth the Queen of England's long-lost gem. I'll be the Howard Carter figure, and you can be my Lord Carnarvon, just like when they found Tutankhamun's treasure chamber."

"But how are we gonna lift five massive stones to reactivate the portal in the first place?" asked

Bill. "Those Orthostats weigh several tons apiece."

"Farmer Scrambles lowered them down, didn't he? We'll borrow his farm machinery to raise them up in the same way. But first, we need to check our speed calculations. With the magnetic force inside the Corridor of Light reduced because of the missing stone, we need to compensate by precisely the right amount. Pass me the knife, quick."

At that moment, the sound of shuffling feet echoed up the chimney, sending a frenzy of fear through Harry and Lou. They eyeballed the shelter entrance nervously. Each was sure that their loudly beating hearts would give them away if a pair of knife wielding crooks appeared. Fortunately though, the foot movements stopped as suddenly as they had started, to be replaced by a faint scratching sound.

The ear-wigging adventurers took their chance to slide down the bank and away. Scarpering up the lane, Lou clasped both hands behind her head and pumped out garbled thoughts.

"Did you hear that? The Ginger Cake Gang admitted that they buried the ruby two years ago, when we thought the police had recovered it. That means, if the gang's safety deposit box was already empty, us finding the key to unlock it was a total waste of time."

Harry's nose twitched and he sniffed before correcting Lou's deduction.

"Not a total waste. I think the gang's lock-up contained some sort of coded guide to the location of the treasure instead of the actual jewel. But if the police retrieved that, surely they would have recovered the ruby by now. It's been two years, I just don't get it."

After puzzling over the fact for several seconds, Harry moved on, positively.

"Never mind that for now. Let's concentrate on the time travel part. If they're telling the truth, it could explain Grandpa Bert's disappearance! What if he didn't die in 1943? What if he walked through this 'Corridor of Light, thingy? Grandpa could still be out there, trapped in another time."

After pausing to consider his own words, Harry drew a final conclusion.

"Well, if those thugs have found some sort of time portal, it must be near the air raid shelters; why else would they be camping there?"

Lou looked scornfully at her brother. "Grandpa trapped in time? You've been watching too much Dr Who. Stan's words can't be taken literally, and anyway, we probably misheard most of it. What he could have actually said was, 'travellING time,' not 'travel IN time.' And when he spoke of the future, he meant next week, not a hundred years from now. I bet 2079 is a set of coordinates on a map, not the year 2079. That makes much more sense. Face it Harry, lifting a few big stones upright isn't going to suddenly create a time machine. Stan's not Ali Bongo the magician; he's just a plain, nasty crook."

Arriving at the car, Lou jumped into the passenger seat and crossed her arms in a huff. A few seconds later, Harry got in quietly, made a quick U-turn and set off home with no more being said on the matter.

Later that day, both siblings sat at the tea table, desperately waiting for their father to arrive. Each was eager to give their own version of the day's events.

To kill time, Harry tried to skewer four sausages at once with his fork, but they suddenly burst apart under the pressure and several bits flew off the table, onto the floor. These were pounced upon by Dirtbag the cat, while Lou collapsed in a fit of hysterical laughter.

"Serves you right for showing off," she tutted. "It was obvious that would happen."

Gathering sausage remnants from the tablecloth, Harry stuffed them into his mouth and threw a fat-chopped smile at his sister in defiance.

Dirtbag was a feral cat, tamed by Harry as a kitten. With a coat the colour of soot, the wild feline was notorious for leaving smelly deposits all around the house. This included inside Mrs Scrambles knitting bag when she left it on the floor one day. From that moment, the cat became

Dirtbag by name as well as dirtbag by nature.

After finishing the sausages, the feral creature went back to playing with a headless mouse in the corner of the room, and then John arrived, carrying a fully piled tea plate.

Rocking back on the legs of his chair, Harry spoke up quickly. "We, err, nipped up to the air-raid shelters, Dad, just like we said we would, and guess who was there?"

John Scrambles looked up suspiciously while chomping on a mustard laced sausage, then imparted a muffled reply. "Whuuo?"

"Stan and Bill, the Ginger Cake Gang. And they're back out of prison," splurged Harry. He related the bunker encounter without mention of time travel, keen to avoid further upset over Grandpa Bert's disappearance, and afterwards, both parents looked shocked. Mrs S insisted the police were rung, and all four abandoned their plates, then filed into the hall. Standing quietly, everyone listened as Sergeant Grinly explained the latest facts to John Scrambles down a crackling phone line.

"It is true, yes. We have released Stan and Bill, in a last-ditch attempt to get the Queen her ruby back. Two years ago, when we opened the gang's safety deposit box using the key recovered by your children, there was no ruby inside, just a folded piece of paper. It was covered in scrawly writing.

Some kind of guide to the ruby burial site, in the grounds of Felton Hall. Unfortunately, the starting point was written in the form of a cryptic clue, which our top code breakers have failed to solve despite two years of trying. Without knowing where to begin, the rest of the map is useless."

Grinly's mournful delivery deteriorated into a tone of desperation as he went on, "We had no option but to set the prisoners free in the hope they'll guide us to the ruby."

A bewildered John Scrambles shrugged his shoulders before speaking back into the telephone receiver.

"So, what you're saying is, those two scallywags are running amok on my farm in the vague hope that they'll lead you to the Queen's missing jewel?"

"That's exactly what we are saying, but have no fear. Last year, when he needed the dentist, we planted a tracking device under a filling in Stan's tooth. The minute the crooks approach Felton Hall, my men will follow. They'll be ready to catch both of them red-handed, digging up the gem."

With the conversation concluded, John put the phone down slowly and turned to Harry who was eager to spill more information, despite having promised himself not to.

"But Dad, they won't catch the Ginger Cake Gang. They are about to escape through a time warp and the police won't be able to follow. We heard Stan talking about it. Their plan is to dig up the ruby in the future and become heroes. All they need do is lift up some sort of big stone blocks to reactivate this time portal and they'll get away scot-free."

John's eyes widened and Mrs Scrambles tutted as Harry added further to the drama.

"If there really is such a thing as a time portal on our farm, I think Grandpa Bert passed through it thirty-six years ago. Accidentally of course. And, if that's true, it could mean he's still out there, alive, but trapped in another time dimension."

At that moment, Lou pushed her brother roughly aside and lunged forward, shaking her head vigorously.

"Take no notice of Harry; he's living in cloud cuckoo land as per usual. The real truth is obvious. Stan twigged we were listening to his conversation and spouted a load of random mumbo jumbo to throw us off the scent. He's making fools of us all. Who believes in time travel anyway? It's total poppycock."

Lou stopped talking, abruptly. She had noticed her father going entirely white in the face and he was rubbing one hand up and down the back of his neck in a clearly agitated state. As John wandered away in a daze, the others followed silently back to the dining room, where John took a deep breath, then turned to address the whole family through a pained expression.

"Unfortunately, Harry's version of events fits in every detail with my memory of Grandpa Bert's strange disappearance back in 1943. We had just found several huge stones lying hidden in the undergrowth, and WE TOO, lifted them upright. It was within minutes of that, that your grandfather vanished forever."

CHAPTER 3.
CRYPTIC CLUES AND NUMBER PUZZLES

"**W**ow," said Harry. "So, tell us the exact sequence of events, then Dad. If Grandpa's not really dead, but trapped in time, we need to understand how it could have happened."

John sank slowly into his chair on one side of the table whilst the others took up positions opposite. Harry and his mother stood open-mouthed in anticipation, while Lou shook her head in denial as the story unfolded directly from John's mouth.

"I've never been a big believer in time travel, any more than Louise here," he began. "That's why I refused to accept such a thing could possibly explain your grandpa's disappearance... Until now."

Pushing back the chair, he hoisted himself shakily upright, gripping hold of the table edge to continue.

"It was one summers evening back in 1943. Grandpa Bert had been directed by the War Office to clear a patch of woodland, ready to build three new air-raid shelters close to the aerodrome. He took the tractor and bale lifter up the green lane to begin the work, and I tagged along. We soon found six large, oblong stones lying flat and overgrown with thick brambles. Your grandpa said they were remnants of a neolithic stone cluster, a bit like Stone Henge; he'd read a book on the subject. They were called Orthostats and thinking the slabs might be handy back at the farmyard, we spent an hour heaving them upright with the bale lifter.

"Your grandpa's idea was to draw a flat-bed trailer alongside each one, lean the Orthostats over and see-saw them onboard. I was sent off to fetch the trailer, but when I got back, your grandpa was nowhere to be seen. Thinking he had gone to check his crops, I loaded the first stone and took it away. Upon my return, he was still missing.

"Of course, I downed tools and began to search properly until suddenly I had to take cover. It was the middle of the war. I could hear the drone of German planes passing directly overhead. One let loose a bomb which missed the aerodrome, but it exploded with a flash in your grandpa's potato field."

John's body curved involuntarily to one side, one arm raised as though shielding his eyes from an explosion, while he relived the experience. After straightening back up, he went on with the incredible revelation.

"Soon afterwards, the area was cordoned off and I was forced to abandon my search. Early next morning, two Redcaps, which is what we called the Military Police during the war, came knocking on our door. Grandpa Bert was to be filed missing, presumed dead. Killed among the potatoes, they said. But it never made any sense. Surely he would have answered my shouts if he had been in that field?.... Well, anyway, with the whole episode a mystery, the only logical conclusion was that Grandpa Bert HAD been caught up in the bomb blast."

John Scrambles fell back heavily into the seat of his chair, shoulders drooping as the childhood memories continuing to flood through his mind. Meanwhile, Mrs Scrambles circled the table and wrapped one arm around her husband, comforting him while he concluded the sorry tale.

"I was devastated, of course, but your grandma, Gladys, being the stoic sort, said we'd just have to get on with things, so we did. Everyone was like that in the war years, I suppose. Plenty of other people's families went missing, not just ours.

"I remember, after the war, Mum would come out with random comments like, 'You'd better get that job finished; I'm expecting your father back soon'. Or, 'We can't let your father come home to this mess, can we?' Those words kept me going. For years both of us lived in the hope that one day, Dad might suddenly turn up. Eventually, though, we gave up on the dream."

John stopped suddenly and raised a wavering finger. He rose to his feet and left the room urgently, returning a minute later with a large, leather-bound book, which he slapped down hard on the table.

"If there's any truth to all that time travel mumbo jumbo, we ought to find valuable information in here. It's one of your grandpa's books on the subject. His interest was the reason we knew what the stones were called in the first place."

Harry and Lou jumped up and rushed around the table to stand behind their father. They craned their necks as he brushed the dust from the leather binding to reveal a dimly written title.

'Neolithic Stone Circles and Monuments of Great Britain.'

After lifting the musty cover, he skimmed through several pages and suddenly began reading out loud.

"In neolithic times, large stones were sometimes cut and then reared up on one end to form a pattern. The blocks were known as Orthostats and a few had bridging stones on top, like those at Stonehenge; others did not. Various geometric formations were common, with a circle being the most popular, and all were located between 50-55 degrees North in latitude. Many were aligned to identify the summer or winter solstice or served ceremonial purposes. They are also believed to have been ritually charged."

John looked up from the book with a wistful expression. "It just so happens that our farm latitude is 52.9 degrees. Pretty much perfect for that sort of thing. But I remember another, smaller book, which I read after Dad's disappearance. It described a slightly different arrangement. A cluster of six stones in parallel rows of three. Some of those rocks were supposed to have powerful magnetic properties, with evidence presented based on cave paintings and ancient scrolls. "John's voice faded. "I must try and find that other book."

He stared at the wall for several seconds, then turned back to address his children. "There's something very mysterious, even sinister about those Orthostats. I've always felt that if we hadn't have touched them, your grandpa would have remained with us. If only I'd have found hard scientific evidence of time travel back then, I would have kept searching, but the truth is it all seemed like a lot of fanciful stories."

"So the Orthostats really could explain Grandpa's disappearance," said Harry excitedly. "Which means, Bill and Stan might actually be telling the truth for once."

A stormy look crossed Lou's face at the realisation that her father was coming round to Harry's way of thinking, and determined to undermine him, she threw her opinion into the ring. "Look. Even if a full set of these Orthostats did form some sort of magnetic time machine, there's no way it could work properly now, with one stone missing, is there? That would mess things right up, wouldn't it?" She looked smugly at her brother and then glanced across at her parents for support.

"It does sound doubtful," agreed Mrs Scrambles as Harry stalked around the table, both hands clasped behind his head in exasperation. After three laps, he stopped and locked horns with Lou again.

"Listen, Louise. Stan admitted that pinching your motorbike is crucial to their plan. He also said travelling at a higher speed along the Corridor of Light somehow makes up for the missing stone. In 1943, I reckon Grandpa travelled into another time dimension at walking pace, and when Dad removed one Orthostat, he couldn't walk back. Since then, we know the Ginger Cake Gang have used the Corridor with only five stones upright. We heard 'em say so. That's how they arrived here. There must be something that compensates for the missing stone, and that something has to be extra speed, I'm sure of it."

"What a load of drivel," bawled Lou. "Where

are your facts to back up this bonkers hypothesis, Harry. Hard evidence, that's what we need, not dreamy theories. Without some sort of proof of how this broken time portal might work again, there's no point in discussing the subject any further."

With that, she banged her hand hard on the table and stormed off. However, like it or not; Lou's head was buzzing with possibilities. She imagined herself zooming between neolithic stones on the trail bike, exploring time zones and saving worlds. What adventures she would have. A moment later, she snapped herself out of it, feeling overcome with annoyance. Harry had almost hooked her in with his crazy time travel theories; all based on Stan's stupid speech, but why should anyone believe the words of a criminal? Lou decided to gather her own evidence. She would destroy Harry's theory once and for all and at the same time, expose what Bill and Stan were really up to. Harry always stole the limelight, ever since turning up on the farm, aged six. Enough was enough. Now it was her turn to get a pat on the back. She would show him up for giving their father false hope. Fancy even suggesting Grandpa Bert might still be alive after thirty-six years. "Pah."

With Mrs Scrambles leaving the dining room at the same time as Lou, Harry took the chance to ask his father a tentative question. It was based on a thought which had been on his mind for several years. "Dad, do you think that your own father's disappearance was part of the reason you adopted me?" John Scrambles hesitated, then nodded slowly.

"Maybe, but it was your mother's idea initially. She thought I'd be the ideal candidate, having grown up without a father myself, and she was right; I did want to give something back. Perhaps to ease the guilt I felt over Dad's disappearance." John smiled weakly, and Harry was once again overcome with a deep desire to resolve the strange case of his missing grandfather, one way or the other.

Meanwhile, in the low evening sunlight, Lou's motorcycle rasped along the Green Lane and noisily passed the air-raid shelters, from where two dark outlines soon emerged. The figures mounted their bicycles, pedalling hard in frantic pursuit of the girl on a trail bike, who slowed to a cruise, allowing the crooks to keep up for several minutes. Suddenly, she accelerated out of view, swerved in a wide arc behind the copse and rode back around to the bunker.

After dropping the motorcycle onto its side stand, Lou ran inside, scanning the walls inch by inch under the light of the flickering fire until her eyes met with two new patches of writing. She pursed her lips in satisfaction. This was just as suspected. The scratchy sounds heard earlier had been made by a knife blade, carving words onto the wall. The writing brought back memories of school algebra lessons, and she rattled off the first three lines without hesitation:

With all six stones present, L equals 5.5555:

52.9-7.9(M) divided by 6 = 7.5

∴ 7.5 x S x L = 100years

∴ S=2.4mph.

After studying this equation carefully, she drew several conclusions:

* 'S' seemed to be short for speed, in miles per hour.

*52.9 was the measurement of latitude upon which their farm was situated.

*M might be to do with magnetism, and L, she suspected, was the effect of light. That would tie in with Stan referring to the portal as a Corridor of Light.

The rest of the first equation rang no bells, apart from the three dots arranged in a triangle, which she knew from maths lessons represented the word, 'therefore'.

Moving on, Lou considered a second calculation, scratched below the first:

With only five stones present, NL = 0.23668

52.9-(7.9(M) divided by 6 = 7.5 -1(RM) = 6.5

$\therefore 6.5 \times NS \times NL = 100$

$\therefore NS = 65mph$

RM must be reduced magnetism, NL, the new effect of light with one Orthostat missing, and NS, new speed, mulled Lou, pulling a notepad from her pocket. It was just as Harry had suggested. Everything written on that wall pointed to what he had said all along. By increasing the speed of travel from walking pace to 65mph, the missing stone could be compensated for and the portal reactivated. Annoyingly, Harry was right, but at least she could save face by providing this new evidence to the others. Harry hadn't thought of exploring the shelter. She was one step ahead of him for once. After copying down each and every line meticulously from the wall, Lou ducked out of the shelter and rasped away on her trail bike before Stan and Bill could return.

The next day, there was no following Harry around, no constant stream of sarcastic comments and no fake interest in the modifications to his car. Instead, Lou spent the morning in her room, and Mrs Scrambles, fearing her daughter unwell, visited several times. On each occasion, Lou pretended to be catching up on homework, when in reality she was busy making sense of Stan's scrawlings.

Finally, jotting her interpretive notes on a separate page in the notepad, Lou ventured downstairs.

Feeling nervous, but equally looking forward to teaching Harry a thing or two about detective work, Lou waited unusually patiently for her chance to impress.

The clatter of cutlery against plates was accompanied by the pungent smell of Stilton cheese as John Scrambles stabbed a large slice with his knife. After dipping the cheese into the mustard jar, he pulled it roughly into his mouth with his teeth, following up with a pickled onion. Then he embarked on a conversation with his mouth still half full.

"Don't forget, Harry. It's your turn to stay with Grandma Gladys for a couple of nights. Her seventieth birthday is coming up soon, and Louise visited last year."

Harry nodded reluctantly and waited for the inevitable chiming in of Lou on the topic.

"Yes, Harry. I hope you enjoy eating lumpy porridge with salt in it. Not to mention the vile pink blancmange and stringy pineapple chunks that Grandma Gladys always serves. While you're stuck with her, I'll be riding Dandy and having fun with my friends Sophie and Rose Smith. They're coming to stay over. Rose has just been to Turkey on a school trip so you'll miss hearing about her adventures for a start."

Harry went red in the face. It was true. He would miss hearing about the Turkey trip, and wondered whether Lou had guessed just how fond of Rose Smith he really was.

Sparing Harry's embarrassment, Lou's mind suddenly flicked back to the time portal, and she cleared her throat loudly.

"On a more important note... I've gathered the evidence that time travel is possible with only five stones, and can confirm that a speed of precisely sixty-five miles per hour will re-activate the reduced portal. As a consequence, I now agree with Harry. Bill and Stan plan to steal my trail bike, scarper into 2079, then dig up the ruby to become heroes and claim a huge reward. Exactly what we heard them bragging about."

With Harry's face displaying a look of utter astonishment, Lou felt euphoric, but two seconds later Mrs S. brought her down to earth, speaking in a stern voice.

"Louise Scrambles. Don't even begin to think that any time soon, either you or Harry will be allowed to go waltzing off through this time warp thingamajig, because I forbid it."

Lou scowled and pulled out the notepad, slapping it down hard on the table.

"Well, here are my calculations just in case anyone besides that pair of raging crooks IS allowed to use the Corridor of Light. Stan etched these figures on the bunker wall, and they demonstrate that the portal works at walking pace with six stones, but requires 65mph with five." Lou stared hard, first at her mother, and then her father, whose expression of cheery enthusiasm had been suddenly replaced by a look of total despair. She stopped talking abruptly as John took over with a distinct stammer in his voice.

"So, it is true. By removing that sixth stone, I trapped my own father in another time dimension. It was me who made it impossible for him to walk back through the portal, however hard he might have tried. Thirty-six years a prisoner, and all because of my actions."

John slumped into his chair, holding his head in his hands while Harry glanced at Lou, signalling the need to raise the mood, before moving things on as optimistically as he dared.

"Look on the bright side though, Dad. Grandpa could have ended up at the bottom of a bomb crater. Getting stuck in another time dimension probably saved his life."

"Yeah, and now we know about the time portal, we can watch Bill and Stan when they fire it up. That will prove it safe so that we can travel in search of Grandpa ourselves and bring him home." Lou squinted at her mother, expecting another negative reaction, but instead the room went quiet. Eventually, John raised his head, managing a half-smile.

"I suppose you're right. Perhaps it was fate," he

conceded.

With the spirits of the entire group lifted, Mrs S piped up with an unexpectedly sensible suggestion.

"But, why can't we just return the missing stone, then walk through the portal like your grandpa did? Why risk hurtling at break-neck speed between two walls of solid rock?" John Scrambles raised his eyebrows to acknowledge his wife's idea before glumly explaining that such a thing could never happen.

"The missing Orthostat now forms the foundation slab beneath my workshop... Dad wanted the thing used, so I used it, in his memory." John watched his wife's eyes roll, and Harry, who could feel the chances of ever finding their grandpa, slipping away, attempted to salvage the situation by buttering up his mother.

"You're right to be cautious, Mum. Speeding through the portal with five stones is risky. We would need to gather more information before trying that out. The other book about stone clusters will tell us more about how the Corridor of Light works. Do you think you could find it, Dad?"

Perking up at the thought of being helpful, John disappeared into his study, and after a lot of banging and crashing, a joyous cry rang out. He hurried back to the others, rambling excitedly, armed with the wide-open book.

"It says here that early cave paintings depicted neolithic man walking between two parallel rows of three Orthostats, surrounded by a brilliant white light.

Furthermore, ancient scrolls suggest that time travel, through a period of one hundred years is possible. Apparently, walking along the corridor at sunrise leads to forwards travel, whilst to go back in time, a sunset stroll is required. The Orthostats must be lined up precisely East to West and the pair at each end of the row need to be made from a rare type of magnetised ironstone called lodestone. The magnetic waves react with sunlight to create a focused energy beam, kept in place by continuous shadow strips, cast by the stones on either side of the Corridor of Light."

"Wow," splurged Harry. "So, magnetic power beefed up by the sun's energy, all trapped in by shadows, delivers the explosive power needed for time travel."

"That's what it says," confirmed John, "And Grandpa used the portal in the evening, which means he will be trapped in the past."

"That's if he's not dead," said Lou, bluntly. This was her attempt at dampening Harry's over-enthusiasm, and it resulted in a prolonged silence, eventually broken by Mrs Scrambles.

"But why would neolithic man have built this sort of time portal thingy in the first place?"

Harry's father ran his finger quickly down the next page in search of the answer, which he read out in a boisterous voice.

"The Corridor of Light was constructed shortly after the last ice age. At that time, lingering winters extended over many years, decimating food supplies. High priests in consultation with astronomers, came up with the time portal idea to allow warrior parties to fetch food. Consequently, by travelling forwards or backwards in time, the mass starvation of their own people was avoided."

"Ahh, that so makes sense, but why stop using it... Ever?" asked Lou.

"Yeah, something like that would be worth a fortune these days," added Harry. "People could fetch a copy of next week's Racing Post and then back all the winners." He contemplated the idea for several seconds before John put him straight.

"In those days, people were only interested in survival, Harry. Pure and simple. Once the weather warmed up after the ice age, the Orthostats were no longer necessary and their significance forgotten. Eventually, they must have become overgrown and lost. Your grandpa was most likely the first person to discover and accidentally activate the portal since neolithic times." He closed the book carefully and pushed it towards Harry. "Give it a proper read if you like, but for now, I've work to do."

With that, John got up and left the room.

That night, Harry went to bed early. He had planned to finish reading his book entitled, 'Wasps and Hornets, Large and Small', before immersing himself in the stone cluster book, but a squeaking door soon signalled Dirtbag entering the room. The feral beast jumped onto Harry's bed, tamping the edge of his pillow to leave a set of dirty footprints, then curled up, stretching out one paw with a yawn. At that moment, a single claw hooked a scrap of paper protruding from a book on the bedside table, and it dropped into Harry's lap.

Harry recognised the tatty bookmark, instantly. The folded paper had been pulled by him from Stan's T-shirt pocket, two years earlier as he searched for the key to the crook's safety deposit box. Harry glanced up at two T-shirts pinned to his bedroom wall and a strong memory flooded back. Bill and Stan had cast aside their fruit juice soaked upper garments after being mobbed by a swarm of angry wasps. This was the result of Harry and Lou pelting fruit at the criminals to attract the stinging insects, a top idea of Harry's amid the battle. The discarded shirts had been kept as souvenirs ever since.

Unfolding the crumpled sheet of paper for the first time, a tingling sensation ran through Harry's body as one particular line caught his eye.

'Felton Hall grounds. Starting point, fridgemaker NWC.'

The sentence immediately hit home as a possible cryptic clue, just like the one described by sergeant Grinly on the phone.

Harry's heart fluttered. Could this be a copy of the ruby map? He was suddenly wide awake and his mind flooded with questions:

How was it that Mrs Scrambles had not thrown away the grubby note in two years, and equally mysterious, why had he never bothered to study its contents at the time or since? The ruby map had survived against the odds as if that were meant to be. Harry tilted his bedside light to illuminate a scrawly jumble of words which resembled a madman's crudely written poem.

'Blue tUesday, Red Insects Every Day

Roses are red, violets are blUe, sugar is Brown, and so are You.'

Below the mad poem, it said,

'Felton Hall grounds. Starting point, fridgemaker NWC

Face NE:

Forward 32 strides, left 6, forward 17, right 21, forwards 11, right 2, back 6

Sideways _ _ _ _ _ _ _ _ _ _ _ _ _ _

Forward _ _ _ _ _ _ _ _ _ _ _ _ _

Bingo.'

The top two lines were easy to decipher. By isolating the random capital letters, the words,

BURIED RUBY appeared. Below, a reference to Felton Hall grounds was clear, but the next sentence was written in the form of a cryptic clue:

"Fridgemaker NWC," he slowly whispered. "Fridgemaker?" Was it an anagram, perhaps?

Harry sat bolt upright in bed and read the note twenty times over, then, after no further breakthroughs, folded the sheet. Rummaging in his bedside cabinet for a pencil tin, he stowed the map safely and allowed his head to drop to the pillow beside Dirtbag.

As Harry fell asleep, his subconscious mind filled with time-travelling dreams and thoughts of recovering the Queen's priceless ruby.

CHAPTER 4.
HARRY'S TURBO INVENTION

T he following day, with the whole family gathered at breakfast time, it didn't take long for the topic to veer from the mundane. Harry passed around the map to blank expressions as each person tried, but failed, to make sense of the jumble of words. Changing the subject, Lou queried the destruction of one of the air-raid shelters.

"Ah, the demolished bunker was down to me," began John, "After your Grandpa's disappearance, the Ministry Of Defence went ahead and built their shelters, one of them right between the Orthostats, but the grassy mound reminded me of a giant grave, so I bulldozed it when the war ended. Recently, I lowered the Orthostats, too. As you kids grew older, I was worried you might climb up and have an accident if you came across them while out exploring."

"Oh, I get it. So the Ginger Cake Gang arrived here through the portal before you laid the stones down," surmised Harry. "Hence, they now need to raise them up again." Lou suddenly took on a bright look and interjected forcefully.

"And more importantly, they're gonna need my motorbike because it's the only thing fast enough to reactivate the Corridor of Light." She paused and looked pensive. "So, why don't we encourage the gang to steal it? Then we can spy on them trying the portal out, like I said before? If it works, we use it ourselves to get the ruby and look for Grandpa." Lou glanced hopefully across the room, but her mother was still having non of it.

"Louise Scrambles, stop right there. If I've told you once, I've told you a thousand times. There'll be no high-speed travelling through any neolithic time-portum, worm hole, thingamajig. Neither should anyone mention any of this to your grandmother. The thought of her long-lost husband being trapped in another time dimension could finish her off. Have I made myself clear?" Mrs Scrambles slammed all four plates together and marched through to the kitchen, but after checking the coast was clear, Harry continued talking in a whisper to Lou.

"If Stan steals your motorbike, though, how will we follow? Rivet will never reach sixty-five, especially over a rubble patch," Harry's voice trailed off as the cogs inside his head whirred ferociously in search of a solution to the problem, and taking advantage of the silence, John Scrambles, who had heard the whispers, entered the conversation.

"Steady-on, your mother's banned time travel, don't forget. I suggest dropping the subject for now. You can do me a favour instead. Take the bale lifter up the Green Lane to the straw stack across from the bunkers. I need to load a trailer tomorrow and I can't drive both vehicles there myself."

The siblings took the suggestion gratefully, soon arriving at the mountain of straw in the loader. After lifting a giant bale from the stack and laying it on the ground, Harry teased the prongs of the straw fork underneath and flipped it on end, while Lou observed from her perch on the tractor's padded toolbox lid.

"What exactly are you doing, Harry?" she asked, "Dad never said anything about moving stuff."

"I'm demonstrating how easily this bale lifter can up-end a large object," said Harry, with a flash of his eyebrows. "And don't look now, but we're being watched." Harry nodded towards the two heads which had popped up over the fallen trunk of a nearby tree. Parking the tractor and switching off the engine, he placed the key rather obviously on top of the sun visor, then climbed backwards from the cab, followed by Lou. They turned around slowly to find the figures gone, and headed home on foot, tracing the line of dry stone walls across country, while Lou voiced her latest set of concerns.

"I know it was me who suggested those scallywags should be allowed to steal my motorbike, but I've decided I don't want them to have it, after all," she said. "If they ride off into the future, I might never get it back!" Harry grinned, then answered reassuringly.

"Don't worry; My plan is for us to tail the crooks in Rivet. We'll easily find the ruby with a copy of the map, then we can retrieve your motorbike and use it while searching for Grandpa. A bike will be much easier to hide than Rivet in 1879. Are we agreed?"

"Well, yeah, but how do we follow the Ginger Cake Gang in the first place? You already said. Rivet can't possibly reach that sort of speed."

"That's why I've decided to soup her up," replied Harry. "By the time I've finished, Rivet will deliver all the speed we need. I just have to iron out a few technical details in my head, first." He descended into a zombie state for the remaining journey, while Lou followed along quietly for once.

At the workshop, Harry raised the car bonnet and jabbed a finger at Rivet's air filter inlet pipe, before turning to face his sister, head-on.

"See that pipe? I can connect to it and turbocharge the engine," he said proudly.

"Turbocharge the engine, turbocharge the

engine with what?" asked Lou.

"With a hair dryer," replied Harry, casually.

"A hair dryer? A hair.... dryer." Lou wafted an imaginary one around her head, while pretending to steer an equally imaginary car with the other hand. "And how will a hair dryer make your car go any faster, frazzle-head?" She turned to rest both palms against the shed wall and banged her head slowly three times on the bricks, but Harry remained resolute.

"If you fetch mum's old dryer from under the stairs, you'll see what I mean. I'll stick a set of new back wheels on Rivet while you're gone. They should help, too."

Lou stomped off, returning ten minutes later with the hair dryer, which Harry quickly gaffer-taped to the engine air intake by the blower end. After connecting the electrical supply cable to a box alongside the car battery, he stood back to admire his workmanship. "I've been dying to turbocharge Rivet for ages. Now is the perfect opportunity," he said, poking a bundle of wires through a hole in the bulkhead to reach a dashboard switch, while Lou tapped her foot sceptically.

"Listen, Scourgeeo; turbochargers are extremely complicated bits of kit. How's a gaffer-taped, Daft Harry bodge-up going to cut the mustard? For a start, hair dryers run on AC power. Not DC like a car does," she said, throwing a dagger glance at Harry, who returned the glare with a knowing smile.

"Ahh, but you see, I've fitted an AC/DC inverter to Rivet already," he said. "And turbocharging is easier than you think... It's simply a case of providing more fuel and more air to the engine. The hair dryer blasts in the extra air and pulling out the car's existing choke lever will add more petrol. Then, BOOM! Off we go through the Corridor of Light. Faster than a baked bean fart."

Lou gnashed her teeth in blind irritation. "So, what's with the new wheels, then? Where do they come in?" she snarled.

"They have a bigger circumference, which means that each wheel rotation moves the car further forward, creating more speed," said Harry. "With the turbo, plus big back wheels, we'll get more miles per hour while still retaining reasonable steering control."

"Reasonable steering control? You say reasonable steering control? We're about to hurtle between massive boulders at break-neck speed. What makes you think that reasonable steering control is enough to save us from getting killed, then?" thundered Lou.

Harry opened the driver-side car door, lolled his head over to one side, and eyeballed his sister across the roof. "There's no point in arguing about minor technicalities. Our biggest problem will be convincing Mum to let us travel through the

Corridor of Light in the first place." Lou grunted an acknowledgement, then began circling the car, cracking her fingers one by one as she went. Finally, after three laps, she stopped and dropped the car bonnet with a bang.

"Well, let's go for a test drive, then," she said. "If Rivet really can go faster, maybe I'll tackle Mum, but I'm not promising anything."

A few minutes later, cruising up the farm track, Harry glanced at the looming storm clouds on the horizon. The rolling grey wall of gloom coincided with the sudden dark veil of trepidation that had come over him as his sweaty hands slid around the steering wheel and a series of random car facts whizzed inside his brain like out of control fireworks. A brand new, Ford Anglia car could reach seventy-four miles per hour over smooth tarmac on a test drive, Harry knew that was true from a magazine article he had read. But with twenty years of engine wear, an extra passenger, and the rough terrain to consider, that top end speed would be considerably reduced. Would his home made turbocharger and big wheels compensate? Gazing out of the window, the rapidly scudding clouds seemed to urge him on and he pulled onto the field, pointing to an object alongside the car.

"We'll use that bird feeder to mark our start position. You watch the speedo, I'll concentrate on driving. As soon as we reach sixty-five, throw this brick out of the window." Harry slapped a half-brick, unexpectedly into Lou's lap from the back seat where he had stowed it earlier, and she nodded silently. Then, pointing both index fingers down the field, she raised her thumbs like a gunslinger touting a set of pistols.

"Okay, let's burn rubber, go go go," she shrieked, performing a heavy drum roll on the dashboard. Harry floored the throttle and locked his bulging eyes onto the field ahead, while Lou squinted at the speed dial as it eased upwards. 30... 35...40, 45...50...The steering wheel began to judder, sending violent ripples through Harry's entire body, but he flicked the hair dryer switch and pulled out the choke, anyway. A sudden WOOSH was accompanied by an obvious surge in performance and Harry began ratcheting himself back and forth between the seat and steering wheel, encouraging the car on, even faster... 55... 56... 57. They were running out of field. 58...59.......62, 64... A drystone wall loomed twenty yards ahead... Lou lobbed the brick and then shielded her head with both arms, expecting a heavy collision. Harry swerved violently and a plume of dust rose high into the air, while loose stones rattled loudly against the car body. He wrestled with the steering in front of the wall, both eyes unblinkingly wide open. Finally, upon regaining control, he casually pushed in the choke, switched off the hair dryer, and cruised back to the bird-feeder. Jumping out, he threw open the car bonnet and began poking at the components, while Lou joined him, sheepishly.

"Everything alright?"

"Everything's fine. A tad warm, that's all." Harry raked his fingernails, nervously, backwards and forwards against the radiator grill. "No leaks or major disasters, and did you feel that power surge? Epic. Told you it'd work. Now let's measure how far we took to reach full speed."

He walked tentatively back down the field, counting each stride as he went... "383, 384, 385, 386... Three hundred and eighty-six yards," he said with a sigh. "That's too far, we have to go faster, quicker. There's a solid, post and rail fence East of the Orthostats and we must start inside that. Rivet won't be up to speed in time.

Lou looked sceptically at her brother. "I told you there'd be no chance with this old crate. My trail bike's the only thing capable of accelerating that fast over rough terrain. It's game over."

"NO..." said Harry emphatically. "We can improve Rivet's aerodynamics. We'll move the paint cans onto the roof, then build an air deflector shield around them and the sunroof." Harry sounded desperate, and Lou took the opportunity to stick in the knife.

"I said cutting a hole in the roof was a stupid idea. The stupidest idea since your last stupid idea, which was bolting large tin cans to the car bonnet... And the one before that, ripping off the aerodynamic front wings. They were all blunders of epic proportion. Frankly, I'm surprised Rivet reached 65mph at all."

Harry's eyes flickered briefly in acceptance of Lou's words before gleaming with renewed determination. "Let's get back to the yard and make the alterations. Then we'll see," he said.

Lou's shoulders dropped. It was clear that no amount of poo-pooing Harry would improve their chances of re-activating the Corridor of Light. Further ranting was pointless. With the notion of time travel hanging by a thread, she felt mega disappointed.

Later that afternoon, back on the starting blocks, Lou stuck her head through the sunroof and waited for Harry's instructions. "Set the deflector shield to forty-five degrees and knock on the roof when you're ready to go," he yelled. Lou dropped the front edge of the tin shield into a slit above the car windscreen, located two hinged props against the back edge of the sunroof, then banged loudly. A few seconds later, the brick landed with a thud, and after measuring the new distance, Lou adopted a smug look.

"And there we have it, as predicted there is no chance of this heap going fast enough," she barked.

"But that's where you're wrong," replied Harry.

"My latest tweaks knocked another forty yards from the run-up, and on the day, we can set off parallel to the wooden fence. Rivet will reach at least ten miles per hour before turning to face the Orthostats. Getting up to sixty-five from a rolling start will be a doddle after that."

"If the speedo's even accurate," snapped Lou in blind irritation.

"Well anyway, let's go check whether Stan's worked out how to use the bale lifter yet," said Harry, eager to avoid any escalation in the argument.

After cruising over to the straw stack and parking out of sight, they climbed onto the car roof, from where Lou shoved her brother violently onto a high bale, and then he pulled her up behind him. Soon; both were thirty feet up on the straw platform.

They looked around in sheer amazement. John Scrambles could be seen in a tractor, three fields away, and beyond; the farmhouse windows glinted in the afternoon sunlight. Finally, after perusing the scene for some time, they dropped to their knees and crawled across the spongy surface towards the front edge of the stack. The grey straw from the previous year's harvest was well rotted and mushy after the winter rains. Toadstools grew in large patches and it was hard to believe that below this top row of bales, the rest were dry and warm. The vast stack provided a multi-storey oasis of cosy winter accommodation for field-mice, rats and many other grateful inhabitants.

Eventually, Lou peered giddily over the front edge and a shiver ran down her spine. On Christmas Eve, two years earlier, she remembered being left dangling from a rope above the Pit of Doom and a fear of heights had haunted her ever since.

With Lou shuffling quickly backwards, Harry picked up the binoculars and squinted through them in the direction of the Orthostats. He immediately noticed four were upright, with the bale-lifter moving clumsily towards the fifth. Its shiny steel tines jerked under Bill's fumbling control and Stan's nasal twang echoed in the wind.

"Down a bit, down a bit, come on. You're all right; you're alright... Wooh... Now lift, lift. Yes, yes, that's it." Stan gave the thumbs up as the final Orthostat crashed onto one end, but then the teetering stone continued beyond the vertical like a giant, wobbling domino. It was set to hammer the next Orthostat along, starting a chain reaction which would obliterate the entire row, and Lou grabbed her head in both hands, yanking her face down into the rotting wet straw. She had no desire to witness this imminent disaster. A shattered row of Orthostats would mirror her shattered dreams. There would be no time travel, no chance of rescuing Grandpa Bert, and no ruby. Lou felt the excruciating pain of disappointment, but Harry merely looked across and chuckled before tapping his sister gently on the shoulder.

"It's okay, sis. Stan tied a rope around the Orthostat to stop it from tipping too far."

Lou raised her head slowly from the fusty bale, spitting damp straw from her mouth as she pursed her lips at the impressive sight. All five Orthostats, now stood proudly upright, bathed in serene sunlight. The Corridor of Light was back in business, and the siblings exchanged broad smiles.

After raising themselves high on their elbows, they continued to spy on the Ginger Cake Gang, who busily cleared away the brambles before performing jigs of joy around each Orthostat.

Both Harry and Lou were overcome by a strange sense of unification with the two evil thugs. It was clear that the time-travelling adventures of all four were about to begin.

CHAPTER 5.
DISASTER IN
THE CORRIDOR
OF LIGHT

That night, Lou purposely left the keys in her trail bike and went to bed. Sunrise was to be 5.30 the following morning.

After a convoluted discussion, the siblings had decided to sneak away from the house without telling either parent. They would watch Stan, and Bill use the portal, then follow in Rivet to perform their own test run of the Corridor of Light, returning before breakfast. Proper pursuit of the crooks and the investigation of Grandpa's disappearance could be undertaken later with a series of regular trips. By then, having proved the Corridor's safety, their mother would surely give full consent.

In their enthusiasm, however, Harry and Lou had forgotten one thing. Any initial trip would necessarily be extended until at least sunset on the same day. And by that time, both parents were sure to notice them gone.

With high levels of adrenaline rendering neither able to sleep, both were fully dressed by 4.30 AM. Before leaving his room, Harry retrieved the ruby map from the top drawer of his bedside table and shoved it into the breast pocket of his shirt. After hesitating, he delved back into the drawer. Shuffling through the jumble of items swept inside by way of tidying over the years. A plethora of small denomination coins, rubbers and ink cartridges met his gaze and a broken length of plastic ruler conjured up a powerful school memory. The measuring device had snapped during the propulsion of a wetted-paper squidgy missile against the music room ceiling. How Harry had collected so much other stuff was a mystery. Several, paper-wrapped bubble gums, three broken watches, two pocket-melted Curly Wurly bars and a brown paper bag containing congealed sherbet pips. Eventually, Harry spotted his St Christopher's medal, which he stuffed into his trouser pocket just as Dirtbag poked his head from under the bed.

"St Christopher is the patron saint of travellers," said Harry to the cat. "He'll keep me safe." Then, after squeezing the bubblegum and sherbet pips into his other pocket, he sneaked downstairs and out into the cold.

With Rivet parked beyond earshot of the house,

a brisk walk was required before Harry could rendezvous with Lou. They exchanged silent nods and got into the lime green car, closing the doors quietly. Harry drove up the lane without switching on the lights and parked out of sight behind the straw stack. Climbing up quickly and silently, the two of them shuffled on hands and knees through the morning mist to the front edge.

The heavy dew, soaked through their trousers, turning their knees red with cold as they waited patiently for dawn, and soon a rich orange glow fanned out across a blue horizon. The life-bringing orb rose majestically into view, spitting raw power, and Harry trained his binoculars on the stone cluster, watching in fascination as the upper tip of each Orthostat was bathed in sunshine. Virgin rays of light spread gradually down the stones and Lou squinted hard, trying to focus before snatching the binoculars from Harry.

"So where is this Corridor of Light?" she snapped. "I don't see anything."

"Give it a chance," said Harry, "The sun needs to rise far enough to cast a strong shadow behind each Orthostat. That's when the Corridor of Light will show up in the middle..."

"Listen," said Lou, putting one hand to her ear and pointing into the distance at a speeding silhouette. The dark outline flashed along the Green Lane, then stopped by the wooden fence where Stan removed his crash helmet. His nasal twang rang out, piercing the cool morning air.

"Look, Bill. The Corridor is forming for us." Lou swerved the binoculars back to the Orthostats, and sure enough, a shaft of visible light now shone brightly between two parallel, shadowy strips. The effect was like a beam of torchlight penetrating a dark tunnel, and Harry leaned across to Lou.

"There's your time-portal, and I reckon we've got about half an hour to use it, tops. After that, the sun will be too high in the sky. Each shadow won't stretch to the next Orthostat along, and light will leak out sideways, reducing the Corridor's power." Lou nodded and switched her focus back to Stan, who adjusted his backpack, then addressed Bill crisply.

"Show me the map one more time before we go, Bill. That piece of paper is our ticket to fame and fortune." Harry took the binoculars from Lou just in time to see Bill wave a piece of paper, then put it away and mounted the motorcycle behind his partner.

After kick-starting the engine, Stan raised one hand and cackled loudly. "It's time for us to go from PORTAL TO IMMORTAL."

Clunking the trail bike into gear, he tweaked the throttle, then released the clutch to send the front wheel high in the air. The crooks accelerated rapidly past the first air-raid shelter with the clank of saucepans accompanying the sharp sound of a two-stroke engine. Eventually, when the pan strings twisted together, the rattling stopped. At that moment, a nauseating hum, rising to a hideous boom, forced the siblings to cover their ears and screw up both eyes, but, desperate to see, Harry prised his reluctant eyelids back apart. He bore witness to an intense X-ray light, which illuminated every bone of the villains' bodies and crackling electrical pulses shot like lightning bolts in all directions. A thick haze of grey smoke drifted across the Corridor to obscure Harry's view, and when the lightning storm cleared, bike and riders were gone.

An eerie silence descended upon the stone cluster as Lou opened her eyes and gulped loudly. She removed her hands from both ears, rotating slowly to face Harry.

"Are you sure travelling along this Corridor of Light thingy is a good idea? Mum'll kill us if we get killed."

Harry nodded a determined nod and climbed down from the bale stack, walking to the car in a zombie state. Climbing in, he gripped the steering wheel and gazed blankly out through the front windscreen. A series of deep breaths gave away the effort spent on preventing his inner thoughts from spilling out in front of Lou... She was right to be cautious. The future was an unknown quantity. Travelling forwards in time could lead to their instant death. A nuclear wasteland may await, or a world filled with murderous aliens. Anything was possible. Harry jiggled his head to send the negative thoughts tumbling from his ears and forced himself to think positive. HE WOULD recover the stolen ruby. HE WOULD make Stan and Bill pay for their ill deeds and HE WOULD find out what had happened to Grandpa Bert, thirty-six years earlier... The tasks were challenging, but luck would be on their side; he was sure of it.

At that moment, Lou opened the car door and climbed silently in. She nodded once, then pointed a single finger towards the Orthostats.

Harry gestured back positively, then tapped the fuel gauge and started the engine. With sweaty palms slipping up and down the steering wheel, he cleared his throat and set off along the line of the old wooden fence. Upon reaching 15mph, he turned towards the Corridor of Light and floored the throttle, while Lou grabbed the edges of the passenger seat with both hands.

"Hang onto your hats," she shrieked as Harry shifted quickly and smoothly through the gears. After hitting 50mph, he flicked the turbo switch, yanked the choke lever and braced both arms against the steering wheel. A second later, sheer force of acceleration flung their heads back and the car met the rubble patch at 60mph.

It was only then that the narrow gap between the enormous standing stones came into focus. The opening seemed barely wider than their wildly swaying vehicle and Harry realised with horror that they were not going to make it through. At the same time, Lou sucked in a giant lung full of air, expecting it to be her last.

Closing both eyes, she waited for them to slam into the first Orthostat, but before that happened, her brother swerved and the back end of the car raked through ninety degrees. The rear wing glanced off the first Orthostat, locking them onto a new and even more deadly course. A head-on collision with the second rock on the other side of the Corridor was now imminent.

Harry wrenched the steering wheel again, and a full-bodied broadside skid flung the driver's door hard against the Orthostat, where the squeal of tearing metal rang out as paint shavings showering in through the sunroof and the vehicle bounced like a bumper car under heavy impact. Harry was knocked violently sideways, his head hitting the side window, but somehow he managed to slam on the brakes, switch off the hair dryer and push in the choke with trembling hands. As the car lurched to a standstill, beads of trickling sweat ran freely down his face and in the sudden silence, Lou slowly wound down the window. Combing back her wet hair with her fingers, she spoke in a croaky voice.

"You bottled it, chicken. And almost got us killed into the bargain!" Harry's response was high-pitched and immediate.

"I couldn't keep the car straight over the rubble. We needed more speed to float us across. I had no choice but to swerve before it was too late." Both siblings fell silent for several seconds.

"Well, I can't say I'm sorry," Lou said, finally and in a calm voice... "It really is game over this time. There's just not enough runway to get Rivet through the Corridor of Light."

"There soon will be," came an unexpected gruff voice from outside the car. Harry and Lou jumped in their seats and twisted their heads like astonished owls.

"Dad! What are you doing here?" Their faces flushed bright red, but the sound of a roaring engine swept away any further feelings of guilt as the bale lifter approached with Mrs Scrambles at the wheel. The amazed siblings leapt from the car, watching as their mother crashed the tractor haphazardly through the fence and deposited the three wooden rails in a heap on one side. Then, as she trundled back towards them, the siblings' father offered some explanation.

"I, er, had a little chat with your mother last night and pointed out that you would more than likely ignore her strict order not to dabble with the time portal. In the end, we both agreed, 'if you can't beat 'em, join 'em. So here we are. We'll be coming along to keep an eye on the both of you." There was no time to argue before Mrs Scrambles climbed from the cab, rubbing her hands together in satisfaction.

"If a job's worth doing, it's worth doing properly," she said. "Now there's plenty of room for Rivet to reach top speed, even with four people inside." Her children were lost for words as she continued impatiently. "Well? Are we ready to go because I haven't got all day to stand around nattering? We've criminals to catch, rubies to recover, and Grandpa Bert to rescue."

"It was your mother's idea to destroy the fence," said John, chipping into the conversation. "But I expect you children to do the repairs when we get back. That can be your penance for keeping us in the dark over the plan. Now, let's get moving before the Corridor of Light vanishes altogether."

With that, he held open the car door for Mrs Scrambles, and she ducked inside.

CHAPTER 6. JUNO

After starting much further back, Rivet hit the rubble effortlessly at sixty-five, the extra weight stabilising the battered car to ensure a neat entry into the Corridor of Light.

Harry glanced at Lou, then eyeballed both parents in his rear view mirror. Identical expressions of steely resignation made it clear that whatever happened next would be dealt with by the whole family, and this feeling left him more than pleased.

Once fully inside the forcefield, the ear-splitting buzz encountered by the siblings from the bale stack, came across as a muffled hum whilst the Orthostats flicked by, one at a time. A split second later, like a flashing camera, the narrow tube of light exploded and serene sunshine shone all around. Harry's heart sank. Had something gone wrong? Rotating his head, a row of strange wooden boxes, supported by long slender legs came into view, and breathing a sigh of relief, he whispered. "No, this is it. We've arrived in the future," then he broke into a broad smile.

Rivet came to a standstill and everyone piled out, their heads twitching uncontrollably as they surveyed the unusual scene. John Scrambles marched over to a nearby field, inspecting its strange crop more closely. The plants were vast, much taller than anything he had ever seen before and such a vivid green. Gasping, he turned his attention to the same peculiar wooden housings that Harry had seen. A long row stretched away into the distance. What could they be, he pondered? Thousands of small birds flew into, then out of the boxes and away across the field.

As Lou strode forward, a fearsome buzzing sent a shudder of recognition through her body, and she tensed, turning to snatch her father's arm.

"They're not birds, Dad. They're monster-sized wasps," she snapped, "Be careful."

"Crikey, you're right, Louise. I can see the tiger stripes now... Everyone move away slowly." Shuffling backwards, John continued nervously. "They are be part of some sort of biological pest control system, aimed at reducing the need for chemical sprays. I think the wasps must harvest caterpillars and aphids from the plants, then feed them to their own larvae in the nest boxes. Let's hope they're busy and don't start bothering us."

John was surprised to notice that Harry had left the group and could be seen crouched on one knee over at the far edge of the copse. As he and the others walked across, Harry stood up. "Tyre tracks left by Lou's trail bike, Dad. Let's follow them to make sure the bandits are out of the way before we set up camp."

All four jumped back into the car, and John manoeuvred his way up through the hole in the roof for a better view of the knobbly tyre tracks. After turning ninety degrees at the top of the field, they followed the markings along a dusty lane, via a gap in the hedge and onto a narrow road where the trail became faint and then disappeared altogether. Harry pulled over, shoved himself up next to his father and swept a full circle with the binoculars, focusing in and out as he went. "I expect Bill and Stan have headed towards Felton. They'd be keen to dig up the ruby as soon as possible and claim their reward," he said.

"Well, they won't come back this way, then," replied John. "So, we can safely set up camp by the Orthostats and take a proper look around after dark. Lou's motorcycle will give away their position and after spotting it we can make plans to steal it back. "For now, though, let's get out of sight. Your crazy frog car sticks out like a sore thumb in broad daylight, Harry. "

Back at the Orthostats, Mrs S pointed to a pair of grassy mounds. "Look! The bunkers have survived all this time," she exclaimed. "Camping inside would be a better bet than pitching a tent outdoors. Harry and Lou, you gather some long twiggy branches to make a broom, and John, I'm putting you in charge of firewood. I'll tidy up in the bunker, but let's unload the car first." They marched over to Rivet, and Harry opened the boot, revealing two bicycles, squeezed inside with their wheels removed, which he lifted out and leaned against a tree.

"Stan and Bill abandoned these, and we thought they might come in handy. Less conspicuous than the frog-car." He grinned at his father and removed a pair of rucksacks from the boot. "Did I see more luggage on the back seat?"

"Yes, we brought our own stuff," said Mrs Scrambles. "Trailing back and forth through an unpredictable time-portal for supplies, struck me as a risky business. Between us we've enough rations for several days, now."

John nodded. "We must spend our time here wisely," he said. "Scouting for the crooks might lead to the ruby if we're lucky, but if we make no progress after two or three days; we cut our losses, grab the trail bike and return to 1979...Agreed?" With no objections, all four adventurers were soon perched on old five-gallon oil drums, eating a hot meal prepared by Mrs Scrambles over a roaring fire. After finishing his food, Harry looked fidgety.

"I think I'll take one of the bikes to reccy the area for new houses, roads and stuff like that. I want to draw an up to date map? A lot must have changed over the last century."

"Okay, but remember," said John. "If anyone asks, you're on holiday in the area, just out for a bike ride. Don't mention our connection to the farm, or things could get complicated. We don't belong in this time dimension and mustn't upset the course of history any more than is absolutely necessary. While you're gone, I'll camouflage the car." He turned to Mrs Scrambles and Lou. "You two, try and get some rest. When Harry and I get back, we'll need you to keep a lookout while we catch up on our sleep."

"But, how come Harry gets to go exploring, not me?" protested Lou indignantly.

"Don't worry, the real action begins tonight. That's when we search for your motorbike," said John, and with his answer seeming to satisfy Lou, each of them set about their tasks.

Harry rode off up the lane, surreptitiously rubbing the breast pocket of his coat with one hand to check for the map before tapping the St Christopher medal in his trousers. At the same time he felt the bag of sherbet pips and, struck by a bout of sugar hunger, pulled over on the bike. Cramming a large handful of sugary sweets into his mouth, Harry's attention switched to the thousands of oversized wasps, swarming just a few yards away. A wave of fear suddenly washed over him and he hastily swallowed the sweets, almost choked, then gasped for air. Recovering quickly, he noticed with relief that despite the sugary aroma, none of the gigantic stinging predators was heading his way. He attempted to rationalise the situation. There must be some sort of invisible barrier to keep the wasps in the field, he mulled. This was the only possible explanation. That fence had undoubtedly saved him from being mobbed by multiple, giant predatory insects, complete with their poison injecting pump guns. Harry pictured a swarm of hostile, six-inch-wasps buzzing around his mouth and shuddered at the thought.

After calming himself, he turned to consider the peculiar wooden housings. Like giant beehives, they were obviously man-made. Each one had an oblong tank suspended by wires beneath it and Harry watched in fascination as several wasps disappeared inside the tank, then re-emerged to enter the nest box above. 'Of course', he thought. remembering the wasp book he had just finished reading. They're water vessels. Wasps mix chewed-up plant fibre with liquid to make a nest-building pulp and also need water for temperature regulation of the nest. The worker wasps fan their wetted wings to cool things down, inside.

Moving on up the Green lane, Harry tried not to look at the wasps again until a huge one suddenly dropped from the swarm and settled on a bare patch of earth at the edge of the field. Feeling compelled to study the lethal insect, Harry got off his bike and edged nervously closer. The pulsating, yellow and black warning marks at one end of the wasp's abdomen, culminated in a gleaming needle-sharp stinger, while at the other end, a narrow waist connected the fearsome beast via wing-bearing thorax to a pear shaped head, where two strong mandibles clicked loudly together like the pincers of a crab. The wasp was nearly six inches long and it seemed to be digging a hole as though about to bury something. However, after creating a shallow crater, the striped insect took off without warning and disappeared into the swarm, leaving Harry bemused.

Turning the corner at the top of the lane, he immediately noticed another significant difference to the world of 1979. There was no aerodrome, no control tower, and no runway or hangars. The entire airfield was completely gone. As Harry wondered what might have happened, a small prefabricated building with a pretty garden came into view. Behind the tiny house, a tall, weird-looking crane was hoisting a massive stone block into the air, though he was not sure why. Reaching into his jacket for pen and paper, Harry marked the changes on a new map just as a girl of about his own age stood up in the garden and waved. She had a cheerful face, partly covered by dark glossy hair, which blew loosely in the gentle breeze. A trowel swung from side to side as she addressed him.

"Hello."

"Hello," replied Harry, going red in the face and launching into an unprompted defensive speech.

"I'm er, on holiday. Not from around here at all... Just happen to be camping... Nearby that is... I'm, err, out for a bike ride, and that's it really...." His voice trailed off nervously.

Camping?" she said. "Don't you mean Glamping? Camping's what they used to call it before solar-powered, triple-walled, inflatable tent fabric was invented. I remember reading about people who camped in the olden days. It was a freezing cold, soaking wet experience, and if the weather finally did turn hot, there was no air conditioning and no fridge, either! Camping must have been horrible. If you really are camping, you must either be a history buff or plain crazy. Which is it?" she inquired, jovially.

"A history buff. Yes, that's what I am. Super interested in all things historical. Particularly anything from one hundred years ago, that's my favourite era. I'm a specialist, in fact." Harry felt pleased. He had stumbled on a great cover story to mask that, having been born in 1966, he would be unable to hold any conversation about the world of 2079.

The girl stepped over a low hedge made of box plants and gently stroked the handlebars of Harry's bike. "Wow, your bicycle is in amazing condition for its age. My hover trike has a broken capacitor and won't even float at the moment. I could do with a set of wheels like yours. Much more reliable. Is that a chain drive?

How wonderful. Anyway, where are you from... Normally?"

"Oh, just up the road," blurted Harry, kicking himself and quickly amending the dim-witted sentence. "Originally, that is... But my family moved away, generations ago. Never been back since... until now. My parents wanted to see where their ancestors came from. That's why we're here. What's your name, by the way?"

"Juno," she said."

"Juno what?" asked Harry. The girl laughed, and Harry clarified the question earnestly. "I meant, what's your surname, that's all."

"No one uses surnames any more, do they?— Oh, I get it, you're doing that history thing again...Well, historically, I happen to know that my great great grandmother was called Rose Smith as a girl, then she became Rose Scrambles by marriage. I found her old passports in a box of trinkets passed down by my mother. The passports dated from the 1970s and 80s when Great Great Nana Rose travelled all over the world. Her first journey was a school trip to the country that used to be called Turkey. She was only fourteen, amazing. I've seen loads of her olden days stuff. It dates back to before the World Council introduced the ten-point plan... You know, when surnames and passports were got rid of."

Harry registered utter astonishment at Juno's

words on two counts. Firstly, the possible family connection between him, Juno, and Rose flashed through his mind... The thought that Lou's friend, Rose Smith, might be his future wife seemed more than surreal. Harry shook his head and blinked twice to remove the idea, then responded to the second of Juno's points.

"The country that USED to be called Turkey?" he asked. Juno giggled again, but straightening her face, explained what she meant.

"The country that used to be called Turkey before the ten-point plan, silly... Since then, the whole world has become a single jurisdiction... A utopian superstate with no borders AND no need for full personal identification... The utopian superstate, originally devised in the year 2025...You must know that date, being a history buff?"

"Oh, yes, of course, but I prefer the older history. Ask me anything about the 1970s or '80s, and I'm your man, but I don't pay much attention to more recent stuff. I'm not really that interested... Perhaps if you taught me a few modern facts, I could tell you what I know about the 1970s in exchange..." Juno nodded and beckoned Harry over.

"Okay, it's a deal. Come and sit down. I'll make us a cup of tea." Harry stepped over the hedge and plonked himself into one of two wicker chairs, listening to Juno rattle on relentlessly.

"My mother's a scientist working in the crop compound over the road. It's a restricted area, and the weather within the fence is enhanced for rapid plant growth. Mirrors in space deflect sunlight directly onto the crops, but the warming effect usually overflows slightly. I've even got an Asian tea bush growing in my garden... I expect you've noticed the giant wasps in the compound, too?" she said, continuing without drawing breath. "Well, they're actually a cross between a wasp and a hornet, called a Warnet, and recently, mum's boss has created a much bigger and nastier species... The Deathmonger wasp. Luckily it's impossible for any insects to escape from the compound, but never mind that, tell me your name and give me an interesting historical fact, seeing as you're an expert... Like, ermm, what type of music was the 1970s famous for?"

"My name's Harry and that's the decade when glam and punk rock first became musical phenomenons," he said, feeling pleased to have risked getting to know Juno. She seemed fun, and it was incredible to imagine that she might be his great-great-granddaughter. Thinking it safe to glean more information, he set up a random question. "Now it's my turn to test you on some older history stuff. "Afterwards, you can test me on modern facts."

"Okay, but I doubt I'll be very good," said Juno as Harry stood up and began circling the garden with his hands behind his back.

"What famous piece of jewellery went missing over one hundred years ago and has never been found, even to this day?" he asked.

"Oh, that's easy. You're just being kind, starting with a question like that. Everyone knows it was the Black Prince's ruby, prised from the Queen's Imperial State Crown and replaced with a lump of strawberry jelly by the Ginger Cake Gang in 1977. That story is in all the history books. The missing gem is said to have been buried in the grounds of Felton Hall, just up the road from here. Apparently, the jewel thieves drew a map to record the exact burial site because they planted it on a dark, moonless night in the middle of nowhere. Unfortunately, they and their map vanished soon afterwards. So the ruby is still out there, somewhere random. In the wilderness, but no-one knows exactly where..."

Harry clapped his hands together in excitement. He was overcome with eagerness to impress, and blurted out his secret without thinking. "Well, it so happens that I've found a copy of that very ruby map." Now it was Juno who looked stunned. She laughed a sort of half-laugh in disbelief as Harry continued. "Trouble is, a gang of criminals have a copy too. And they're about to dig up the ruby and become famous celebrities. I want to get there first, but that means deciphering a cryptic clue to reveal the map's starting point. Unless I succeed, the crooks will find the ruby.

Juno looked at Harry sceptically.

"Crooks? Criminals? Really? You've been reading too many history books, Harry. There are no crooks or criminals these days. The superstate caters for the essential needs of everyone throughout the entire world. It is no longer necessary to steal other people's possessions. That's the whole point of a utopian society. Good try, though; you nearly had me going for a second."

Somehow Harry's unflinching expression left Juno desperate to believe his story, however unlikely, and she asked one further question. "So, what makes you mistrust these men, then?" Harry hesitated. He needed to think quickly. The answer must not reveal the truth. His father had warned him about upsetting the passage of history. One slip-up could have serious consequences.

"I've been doing historical research, that's all," he mumbled. "I found that, one hundred years ago, the original ruby thieves disappeared and therefore went unpunished. The two men I'm talking of are their direct descendants. Bill and Stan are their names. They've recently acquired a copy of the map, along with a diary containing hints to decipher the cryptic clue and find the starting point on the map. It's not right that these men should become famous or reap a reward for rediscovering the gem that their own ancestors stole in the first place, now is it?"

"I see what you are saying, Harry," said Juno, supportively. "Okay, so, if you really do have a copy of this map, maybe I could help you solve the cryptic clue. Then you'd become an 'A' list celebrity, instead of them. Just imagine digging up the ruby after all this time. You'd be a mega star. A king of the hyper-screen. Famous beyond measure...And at least you'd have earned it, fair and square."

Harry wasn't sure what to say next. Juno was full of positivity, but his mind swirled with uncertainty. Should he reveal the truth to his great great granddaughter or instead, distance himself as quickly as possible to avoid upsetting history? After some deliberation, Harry decided to go ahead and enlist her help, but only as a friend.

"I don't want to become famous, but I do want to prevent Bill and Stan from being showered in glory when they don't deserve it," he said, pulling the map from his pocket and holding it out. Juno stared hard into Harry's eyes as she took the sheet of paper from his twitching hand and sniffed it.

"Doesn't smell very old, but it's certainly crumpled enough, I'll give you that," she said.

"That may be because I put it through the washing machine by mistake," admitted Harry, coyly.

Juno laughed a confused laugh. "Now I know you're joking. Washing machines were phased out years ago. These days, clothes are self-cleaning under the action of direct sunlight." She unfolded the map and looked at the words scrawled onto the page. "Mmmm. **'Felton Hall grounds, starting point, fridge maker NWC'**... That's the cryptic bit, I presume?" Harry nodded.

Juno rocked from side to side, turning on her ankles and stroked a fingertip gently back and forth across the top line of the map as she closed her eyes in concentration. After some time, she looked across at Harry. "How about this for an idea then? Felton Hall is an old stately home. Perhaps the phrase, fridge maker, is connected to the history of the place. NW sounds like the point of a compass, and C could mean corner.... like — north west corner— History is your strong suit, Harry. ...All YOU need to do now is work out what the words fridge maker might mean in a historical context. I know you can do it, COME ON."

Struck by the similarity of Juno's thought processes to his own, and impressed by the new idea, Harry began to consider the historical angle. A world of possibilities flooded his mind, and after racking his brains for almost a minute, he stabbed a finger triumphantly in the air.

"The Felton Hall fridge. That's it. There was no such thing as electricity when the hall was built. Food was kept cool with ice. That ice was stored in ice-houses found in the gardens of stately homes like Felton. I know the precise location of the icehouse at Felton Hall, so, thanks Juno, you've been a big help."

Harry retrieved the map and smiled broadly. "I'd better be going now. Mum and Dad'll be wondering where I am."

"Glad to be of assistance," said Juno, jumping to her feet. "But hang on a minute, I'll fetch a book about the rise of the utopian superstate. You might like to brush up on a bit of recent history. Pop it back in a day or two, and I'll test to see how much you've learned. We'll probably get around to that cup of tea I promised, too." Harry nodded, and after tucking the book into his jacket, he scissor jumped the box hedge, picked up his bike and rode off, giving a wobbly backwards wave.

Back at the camp site, he was met by the sound of Lou's voice, shouting from the top of one of the bunkers.

"Where've you been for the past three and a half hours?" Harry dismounted and parked his bike against a tree, then ran up the bank, slouching down on the warm grass beside his sister.

"I met a girl who helped me work out where the start point for the ruby map is... her name is Juno, and she also lent me a book on modern history which should prove useful for brushing up on what's changed over the last hundred years." Harry pulled the book enthusiastically from his jacket to show Lou.

"Ooh... A girl...Called Juno... Three hours? Sounds like a big-love-job to me." Harry refused to rise to the bait. He would not reveal his true relationship with Juno. Especially when it was clear that Lou's motive for teasing was envy. He chuckled and got up, wandering off to look for a place to rest.

A little while later, awoken by the smell of food cooking on an open fire, Harry felt immediately hungry. Baked beans heated in their cans and bread, toasted over open flames provided a tasty meal before John led them to Rivet, hidden by several branches. A minute later, Harry started the car engine and Lou rose into the shotgun position, pushing herself up through the sunroof. "You'd better take the deflector shield down; the headlamps are behind it," shouted Harry. After uncovering the spotlights, they blazed a trail to the point where the motorbike tyre marks had faded earlier, and from there, on towards Felton village along dark and deserted roads. "Anyone noticed any more changes since 1979?" asked Harry, looking at Lou, who answered quickly.

"No telegraph poles, no pylons, and hardly any vehicles on the road, but at least that means we're less likely to be seen."

"The aerodrome's vanished, too," added Harry, "And there are no aeroplanes in the sky, either. It's as if no one does flying any more... Juno told me that today's people don't need passports and climate is controlled by huge solar mirrors.

Apparently, the entire world has been turned into a utopian superstate, whatever that means." Their father expanded on the subject, helpfully.

"Utopia is a place or state of being in which everything is supposed to be perfect. From what you've said, it could explain the climate control thing and the giant wasp's, too. Wasps are natural predators, they can be used to control other insect pests instead of relying on horrible man-made insecticides. That idea would be deemed perfection in terms of food production."

"Umm," said Harry, "I'm not sure replacing horrible insecticides with equally horrible, giant predatory wasps ought to be deemed utopian, at all. Ordinary sized wasps can pack a nasty punch if you get on the wrong side of them. Imagine these giant Warnets on a bad hair day, attacking en-masse and armed with oversized, venom-filled pump guns."

Approaching the edge of the village, Mrs Scrambles suddenly tapped on the side window. "Stop the car; I saw something." Harry pulled over, and she tip-toed across the road, disappearing through a gap in the hedge. A minute later, piling back into the car, Mrs S clicked the door shut quietly... "Your motorbike's over in that field, Louise; I caught a glimpse through the gap as we passed by. Let's park out of sight and have a snoop around."

Harry reversed the car a little way up the road

and pulled over. A large cloud covered the moon, and it began to spit with rain as Mrs S guided them through pitch blackness to the trail bike, which was propped on its side stand in the field.

"There's a cottage over there. I wonder if Stan and Bill are inside?" whispered Lou, pointing to the back-lit window of a nearby building.

As they crept closer, the moon popped conveniently back out from behind the cloud to illuminate a pair of twisted chimneys. The building was a tied cottage belonging to the Felton Hall estate. Its curtains hung wide open, exposing three upright figures standing in a huddle by a grandfather clock. The stocky and lanky outlines of Bill and Stan were instantly recognisable, and a third man smiled cheerfully as Stan waved a piece of paper in the air. Bill was dressed in a futuristic smock, and nodded in a business-like manner towards the unknown man. None of the Scrambles family could hear the conversation, but it was evident that the ruby map was being discussed.

Harry signalled to the others to stay hidden and snuck far enough forward to gather the gist of the conversation. Stan was giving a fictional account of how he'd found the map inside an old marmalade jar in the corner of a potting shed on a neighbour's farm. Bill added that his own, comprehensive historical knowledge had been an invaluable aid in deciphering the cryptic clue. The smart man moved towards the window, flashing a

National Thrust badge bearing the name Zackery, and as he listened to Stan and Bill in wide-eyed amazement, the lying crooks continued to embellish their story.

At that moment, Zackery turned his back, allowing Harry to move even closer. He could now hear the full conversation as Stan offered to retrace the directions on the map in full public view, suggesting that revealing the ruby in this way would be a good advertisement for the National Thrust.

"Well, what an exciting story you tell. And it fits in every detail with the known facts. Almost too good to be true after all this time," said Zackery, swooning as he sandwiched Stan's right hand between both of his and shook it enthusiastically. "Digging up the long-lost, Black Prince's ruby in front of an audience will make you both enormous celebrities. Please allow me to contact the National Thrust head office and arrange a media team visit for a couple of days time. Video-streaming the entire magnificent process of you gentlemen unearthing the ruby would clearly be mutually beneficial."

Holding his hands aloft as if heralding divine beings, the man adopted a dreamy tone. "Just imagine the public interest. Two modern-day heroes, retracing the steps of heinous criminals to recover the world's largest and longest-lost gem. The glorious ruby being finally reunited with the

Imperial State Crown as its rightful centrepiece... What a publicity stunt..." With that, Zackery lowered his hands and also his voice. "Of course, the ongoing promotional and video rights, worth a pretty penny will be yours to keep, along with the substantial reward. The live event itself will be sufficient for us to promote the National Thrust and Felton Hall."

Harry peered cautiously over the window ledge, just in time to see Stan, grinning the grin of a man at the pinnacle of his miserable existence, before edging away into the darkness.

Rejoining the others, they travelled back to the air-raid shelter, where Harry filled everyone in as they warmed their hands around a roaring fire.

"Sounds like we've got a couple of days, tops, to find the ruby ourselves," said Lou. "You'd better tell us about this idea of Juno's. We need to identify the start point of the map, quick sharp." Harry rocked back and forth on his tin drum and answered casually.

"It was to do with the fridgemaker wording."

"Come on, then, spit it out. So, what does fridgemaker NWC mean?" Lou snapped.

" Juno suggested that I think historical, and that's when I realised the words fridge-maker might refer to the Mirror Pond by the icehouse. You see, although it only appears to be a decorative feature, actually the shallow pond has an important function. It acts like a giant puddle, freezing regularly during winter. In the olden days, ice was skimmed off and tipped into a nearby underground icehouse, which acted like a giant fridge before electricity was invented."

"So what?" exclaimed Lou.

"Well, the Mirror Pond is what made the fridge work... So, the pond is the fridgemaker. And, being oblong, it has a distinct north-west corner, too... Which is the true start point for the other directions on the map..."

As a look of enlightenment spread across Lou's face like a lightning bolt, she poked the fire in sheer annoyance. Trust Harry to fathom that out, she thought as Mrs S jumped to her feet, beckoning the others enthusiastically.

"Okay, what are we waiting for? Let's go and dig up the ruby before the Ginger Cake Gang get their despicable hands on it," she screeched, heading for the bunker entrance. Harry, however, remained firmly seated, staring at the others mischievously.

"You may as well sit down, Mum; we'd be wasting our time," he said.

"What do you mean, wasting our time?" snapped Lou. "Do you know where the ruby is or not, Harry?" Harry stood up and plunged both hands deep into his jacket pockets. Eyeballing the other's one by one, he slowly withdrew a bright red object and suddenly threw it towards Lou, who lunged to catch it with a screech.

"Lookout, I nearly dropped it... A gobstopper? What's the big deal, Harry?"

"Oh, that's just something for you to suck on while I explain about the ruby," said Harry. Lou threw him a dagger glance while popping the sweet into her mouth and sucking off the top layer. She watched Harry suspiciously as, with a grin, he removed his other hand from the jacket in the manner of a magician plucking an egg from behind an ear and held something up in front of the others. The shiny object flickered in the firelight as slithers of deep red colour danced against the bunker's concrete walls and Harry addressed his mother.

"This is for you, Mum," he said as Lou spat out the gobstopper with a cough.

"The ruby?" she spluttered.

An astounded Mrs S took the gleaming gemstone from her son and placed it onto the palm of one hand, prodding it suspiciously with the tip of a finger.

"Is it real?" she asked, sniffing, then pursing her lips in approval.
"Here, John, you check." Mrs S passed the object carefully to her husband, who turned immediately to Harry.

"Don't worry, son, I believe you," he said, grinning. "When did you dig it up?"

"Right after Juno helped decipher the cryptic clue. I nipped to the edge of Felton village on my bike, cut across the park to the Mirror Pond and followed the directions on the map. The ruby was buried eight inches deep inside a plastic Tupperware sandwich box. I've replanted the Tupperware, of course. Wouldn't want to be accused of stealing something that didn't belong to me. Especially Stan's lunch box." Harry grinned briefly, but then a look of frustration crossed his face.

"Now we have the ruby back, and know where Lou's motorbike is, it is almost mission accomplished, but I do want to witness the Ginger Cake Gang digging up the empty sandwich box amid a media frenzy in a couple of days time. It's the least we deserve after all of our efforts. Those crooks need to be humiliated, it's the only way they can be punished for their crime."

"But what about the ruby? What do we do with that?" asked Mrs S. "None of us can hand it in. Technically we don't exist. And taking the ruby back through the portal would change history, too."

Harry nodded. "You're right on both counts, Mum; but I've worked out a plan to get around the problem. I'll fill you in later, but for now, you and Dad may as well grab the motorbike tomorrow and head home on that. We've achieved everything we came here for. Lou and I will stay one extra day to claim front row seats at the Mirror Pond. If we hide among the trees around the icehouse, no one will even know we're there." Harry looked hopefully at both parents.

"But something terrible might happen to stop you coming home afterwards?" retorted Mrs Scrambles in a frantic voice.

"What could go wrong, Mum?" interjected Lou. "We know the portal works fine, and one way or another, we have to drive our two vehicles back separately. One more day won't make any difference." Lou put on her best sweet look for the benefit of their mother and waited for a decision.

After eyeing John, who nodded affirmatively, Mrs S shrugged both shoulders and capitulated. "Well, alright, but only if you promise to come straight back home after the event. We've still got your Grandpa Bert to rescue, don't forget."

"We promise, Mum. We're desperate to find Grandpa, too," said Harry, moving the topic on quickly.

"Oh, and, can I borrow your camera, Dad? I want to take Polaroid pictures of those scallywags opening an empty lunch box, that's all." Amused expressions spread quickly around the shelter as each of them pictured the scene and they spent a further happy hour reminiscing over previous encounters with the Ginger Cake Gang.

Finally, with the fire dying down, everyone

climbed into their sleeping bags and fell asleep in seconds.

CHAPTER 7. THE TEN POINT PLAN

Harry awoke early the following day. After propping himself against the shelter wall, he picked up Juno's book and began reading about the radical changes, which had occurred over a sixty year period in pursuit of the utopian ideal. The basic ideas seemed pretty cool, he thought, rolling onto both elbows and flicking his feet as he continued.

The book outlined the search for a perfect world, triggered by high levels of war, terrorism, pollution and global warming. Mass population movements had sparked the spread of disease throughout the world and the final straw was a deadly pandemic, beginning in 2019. This brought about the collapse of world economies until the virus was finally brought under control in 2024.

Afterwards, a new world council was formed to prevent society from returning to its old ways. The concept of a perfect utopian society had been born. Crime, poverty, starvation and conflict were to be banished, and over the next twenty-five years, a worldwide plan was implemented in two phases:

World Council, ten-point plan for a utopian society.
Phase one, beginning 2025

1. Large mirrors, launched into deep space, will reflect or direct sunlight, controlling the world's climate.

2. Unilateral disarmament, followed by the decommissioning of all weapons by the year 2050.

3. A total ban on the burning of fossil fuels.

4. Industrial areas and mass transport systems to be fuelled by concentrated solar energy, using the mirrors to meet the high power requirement.

5. The installation of mechanical battery towers to provide a chemical-free, environmentally friendly, power backup system.

6. Introduction of a single currency and universal basic income, with all previous coinage being withdrawn.

7. Income tax to be scrapped and replaced by a value-added tax on purchased goods, applied at tiered rates. Essential food, medicine and healthcare products will be charged at zero, with the levels of taxation rising as goods or services become more luxurious.

8. The development of a plastics-digesting microbe, capable of reducing all types of plastic to a soup for recycling into new plastics or safe

absorption within the environment.

The following chapters went on to explain that the implementation of phase one meant that there would no longer be any need for long-distance travel or migration. The control of weather around the world would improve living conditions everywhere. Previous desert areas and swamps could now grow a wide range of food products. However, as Harry read on, he developed the distinct feeling that the utopian vision seemed too good to be true, and his scepticism increased as problems with the new system started to be described.

After phase one, an explosion in world population had made it necessary to further enhance crop yields. Furthermore, there was an unforeseen problem, caused by the demise of fossil fuels. A reduction in atmospheric carbon dioxide led to a rising proportion of oxygen in air, unexpectedly benefiting species with poor lung efficiency, like insects. As a result, the insects grew bigger and proliferated, causing devastation to plant life. Improved pest control measures were desperately needed to maintain an adequate food supply for mankind, but utopian policy frowned on the release of any chemical pollutants into the environment. To solve this problem, phase two of the plan was implemented, ten years after phase one.

Ten-point plan Phase 2:

9. The construction of specialised, secure farming compounds, protected by double-walled, high-frequency sound barriers. Inside the compounds, high yielding, genetically modified crops could be grown with increased resistance to disease and improved ability to compete with weeds. In addition, biological pest control by genetically modified predatory wasps will allow maximum ethical food production in an ecologically sound way.

10. In conjunction with point 9, a worldwide ban on weedkillers and insecticides shall be introduced to protect the environment. Areas outside the crop compounds will be allowed to run wild, according to the rules of nature, for the benefit of the world.

When Harry finally snapped Juno's book shut, his eyes were wide with astonishment at the high level of human interference in nature. He harboured an uneasy feeling in the pit of his stomach. It seemed to Harry that the so-called utopian world had left itself wide open to possible catastrophe. After shaking Lou awake and filling her in quickly, they held an animated discussion on the topic.

"Imagine if there was an escape from the compounds and hundreds of monster wasps were free to swarm around your jam sandwiches at every picnic," said Lou, as Harry rolled his eyes and raised another point.

"I was wondering how the crops inside the compounds get planted and harvested? Humans can't be involved; that would be way too dangerous. They must use robots."

Lou shrugged and climbed slowly out of her sleeping bag. "Maybe," she said, sniffing her armpits. "Paw... I need to wash..." With that, she disappeared outside in search of soap and water.

Half an hour later, eight rashers of bacon and four sausages sizzled in a pan as John outlined his plan for recovering Lou's motorbike. "I think our motorcycle rescue expedition will require the input of three people. One to keep a lookout in each direction while a third snatches the bike. If we ride there on the two bicycles, I could give you a seater," he said, looking at Lou. "Then you could bring the motorbike back. Are we agreed?" Lou nodded.

"Sure. I'll go with you and mum. Harry's desperate to visit his new girlfriend, anyway. He's even lined up a book to return. Very convenient," she smirked.

A few minutes later, Harry ambled off up the lane, eyeing the crop compound with a new sense of fear and respect. He immediately noticed the pairs of slender poles, arranged one inside the other at the field corners. More posts skirted the field in between, like long wispy fishing rods with thin tips swaying gently in the breeze. Harry acknowledged their purpose out loud. "Radio antennae for creating the high-frequency forcefield around the compound."

At that moment, a particularly loud buzz drew his attention, and screwing up both eyes, he picked out a single, monster predator, hovering at the edge of the crop. The fearsome, yellow and black striped Deathmonger wasp curved its venom-filled pump gun as it dropped onto a large caterpillar and injected its prey before carrying the paralysed insect away. Harry squirmed at the thought of multiple carnivorous wasp larvae in the nest, consuming the helpless caterpillar while it was still alive.

Moving across to the far side of the lane, he attempted to distance himself from the predators, however, the reverberating deadly hum inside his head refused to go away. The noise actually seemed louder now. So real, in fact, that Harry suddenly spun three-sixty degrees in panic. Spotting a flying silhouette above his head, and fully expecting an imminent giant wasp attack, he attempted to scream, but nothing came out. With a throat dry enough to split, both eyes focused intently on the shape until it disappeared into the trees a few yards away. Harry regained his composure, but a moment later, a sense of intrigue took over, and he edged nervously towards the copse, determined to check up on what he thought he had just seen.

After battling through the dense outer bushes to reach a grassy glade, a squawking crow suddenly took off from the ground, and he breathed a deep sigh of relief. A rotting rabbit carcass, the object of the crow's attention, lay before him. Surely this bird was what he had just spied in the air? Beyond the dead rabbit lay the bloodied corpse of a freshly killed young fox with several chunks of raw flesh hanging from its body.

Yuk," said Harry, skirting the animal to reach a pile of clean bones a little further on. He picked up a long stick, poked the skulls of a squirrel and a shrew, then stroked his chin. The small rodent deaths were understandable, but the fox? It was a predator itself, so, what had led to the violent demise of the fox? Ordinarily, Harry would have picked up the clean skulls for his collection, but feeling sure that Juno would be less than impressed, he ignored them and hurried back to the lane.

Up ahead, the shining roof of his new friend's house came into view, and he noticed the bright sunlight reflected from a row of shiny spinning discs fastened to the ridge. Every roof tile also gleamed as though made of glass. Next, his focus fell upon the towering crane, partly obscured by the house. A huge horizontal arm, lifted a giant concrete block majestically towards the top of a vertical stack of similar, interlocking slabs which surrounded the crane's latticed central framework. Harry stood mesmerised as three more blocks were added to the tower. 'A battery backup system', he mused, staring at the feature which resembled a church spire, rising high above the tiny house.

"Hello Harry," came Juno's shrill voice a few seconds later. "You've come back for that cup of tea, then? Where's your bike today?"

"Oh, I fancied a walk...More time to take in the sights. Your crane's impressive," said Harry, stepping over the box hedge onto a neatly mown lawn.

"The battery? Every house around here has one to store excess renewable power. Solar or wind energy builds the tower, then later, the blocks are lowered one by one, converting gravitational force to mechanical energy. This drives a generator, providing electricity that way," explained Juno as Harry scratched the nape of his neck.

"I knew that, of course. I was just saying... Never mind... Yes, I would love a cup of tea."

Ten minutes later, they sat together on the lawn, sipping Juno's home grown Assam tea, which had a wonderfully sharp tang. Harry enjoyed the drink so much that he remarked on it, but Juno's answer was far from expected.

"The flavour comes from my own tea bush, the one I told you about," she said. "I feed it with composted dead Warnets. The peptides in wasp venom give the drink a lovely kick." Harry almost spat out a mouthful of tea but somehow managed to gulp it down. "Anyhow, what have you been up to since yesterday?" continued Juno.

"I read your book from cover to cover, for a start. Fascinating it was, too. I especially liked the chapter on biological pest control within the crop compounds using the predatory Warnets. But I'm a bit worried about the even bigger and scarier Deathmonger monster wasps you mentioned. What if there was an escape? Those critters could seriously sting people," stated Harry in an alarmed tone, taking the history book from inside his jacket and passing it over.

"Well... That's just what Mum's been saying, and she keeps trying to tell her boss, Dr Shizzle. He controls all crop compounds worldwide. Five years ago a group of his scientists crossed the Warnet with a Tarantula Hawk wasp then genetically modified the offspring to develop the Deathmonger, the world's most aggressive insect. It's an apex predator, top of the food chain. Nothing hunts the Deathmonger, so you are quite right in calling it the monstrous Deathmonger. This wasp is so big, it is capable of taking out animal pests, too. One sting will paralyse a rat or a bird in mid-flight. The Deathmonger truly pedals death. AND it can see in the dark because it is partly hornet and they hunt at night. Not even the bats are safe. Mum says Dr Shizzle is oblivious to the risk. He has created nature's ultimate killing machine, but seems totally unaware."

Harry went quiet, but inside, his head was a scramble. To breed a jumbo-sized, swift flying predator, armed with a deadly sting, seemed complete madness, whether locked inside a secure compound or not.

"But, how can this Shizzle fellow believe that his creation is a step towards a perfect world?" he said despairingly to Juno, who nodded her head in furious agreement.

"It's crazy, I agree, but World Council policy states that all forms of biological pest control are ecologically sound and can be considered safe. The Council see no danger because the Deathmongers are permanently constrained within compounds. And what's more, the boffins insist there is no possibility of escape. They swear their twin-walled safety fence is impregnable to all insects." Harry's jaw dropped wide open and massaging his furrowed brow between finger and thumb, he addressed Juno in a reluctant voice.

"But what if I've already seen a Deathmonger outside the compound, though?" These shattering words reverberated around Juno's head, and now it was her turn to suffer from a dropped jaw.

"You can't have... Are you sure, Harry?" she asked meekly.

He related the story of the carcasses in the copse, and then Juno took over in an angry voice. "Mum has always said that one day there'd be a breach of the perimeter fence. She also warned it would lead to the Deathmongers spreading throughout the world. The biological control department simply refuses to listen. Chizzle is obsessed with his precious genetic modifications. He sees himself as delivering the perfect utopian solution for the shortfall in world food production."

After calming herself down, Juno attempted to rationalise the possible sighting.

"Okay, let's say one of those monstrous Deathmonger wasp did somehow pass through the inner fence. It should have been stunned and would then have dropped between the two barriers. The central buffer zone is patrolled twenty four hours a day by drones and any wasps found are returned to the compound. The outer barrier operates at a much higher frequency. It is impenetrable to living insects. Both fences are effective to a height of twenty thousand feet, and wasps can't survive that high up. Therefore, escape is impossible... According to Chizzle."

"That may be true, but what really worries me is that wasps are smart and socially organised," said Harry, frowning. "They have communication skills based on body movement and pheromone release. If a single wasp did find a way out and then returned to pass on the information, a trickle of escaped Deathmongers would soon become a flood." Juno lowered her voice as though worried about being overheard by an intelligent insect.

"But why would the Deathmongers want to escape? The insects inside the compound are bigger and juicier than outside because of the lush crops they feed on. And with animal pests on the menu, the Deathmongers can't be going hungry—can they?"

"No, but what if they've developed ambition? Maybe the Deathmonger wants to proliferate their species. Spread beyond the barriers of their incarceration. Colonise the planet." He leapt to his feet urgently. "We must face this situation head-on. I'll take you to the carcasses. See what you think. I may be completely wrong." Juno nodded and tried to remain optimistic.

"Perhaps what you heard was the buzz of a regular Asian giant hornet. I've seen a few in the area before. They survive in warmer pockets of air, close to the compound. That type of wasp is nothing to worry about in comparison with a monster Deathmonger; believe me — Yes, I'm sure that's what you saw," she concluded.

Setting off along the lane, Harry found himself chewing the inside of his bottom lip as a wave of fear mixed with intrigue washed over him. He took his mind off things by firing more questions at Juno about the crop compounds, which she answered comprehensively. "The mirrors can reflect strong sunlight directly into the compounds even in winter. Crops grow fast and large. As a result, yields are twenty times those of fifty years ago. This frees up land outside, which can be left to nature. The basic concept is excellent. Intensive crop compounds have been rolled out worldwide, ending starvation. Each compound is split into four strips which are planted in sequence by robots. After harvesting the first strip, the robots move the wasp housings down the field to a new growth area. This continuous process allows four crops to be harvested per year."

"And the wasps breed all year round?"

"Oh yes, they do. With no winter frosts, each Deathmonger queen survives for about a year, eventually dying of old age after laying a batch of royal eggs to be reared by worker wasps into new queens. These carry on expanding the system of nests."

"Is the compound already full of Deathmongers?" asked Harry, his mind reeling at the thought of the speed with which deadly wasp numbers could multiply under this regime.

"No. The scientists have replaced the Warnets gradually. It's about half and half at the moment, although, recently, lab technicians have begun collecting thousands of Deathmonger queens ready for shipment to other compounds. The species is on the verge of a massive expansion. An initial ten nests will soon be established in each and every compound around the world." Juno paused, and they walked on in silence for a couple of minutes, absorbed in their own thoughts. Finally, Harry shared still more chilling concerns over the issue.

"But, what if the information on how to escape has already been passed to the new queens? Delivering them to secure compounds across the planet would be like sending killers to prison with their own room key. AND, each monster Deathmonger queen would have the capability to breed a huge army within weeks."

Noticing the mortified look on Juno's face, he changed the subject quickly.

"So, how do you get about, now that your hoverboard's broken? Has your mum got a car?"

Juno looked relieved and giggled before answering, "Is this another of your tests? Cars were phased out years ago. The roads are mainly used by maintenance vehicles, nowadays. Everyone else travels by solar vacuum tube. We can go to town in one if you like. The museum has plenty of vintage cars on show. We can look at those." Smiling back at Juno, Harry pointed tentatively to a small spinney up ahead.

"Over there. That's where I saw the carcasses." They struggled through thick undergrowth until, brushing aside some low branches, the rotting corpses were revealed. Moving further on, Juno looked increasingly uncomfortable and began scanning the air around them, nervously.

"I think we should go now," she stammered, but just then, a loud clicking sound stopped them both, dead in their tracks.

Harry flicked a finger up against his lips, "Shhh!" He sneaked forward, leaned against a tree, and peered around the trunk. The clicking had been replaced by a slurping sound, reminiscent of a child draining the last drops of milkshake from a glass through a straw. A few feet away, a colossal Deathmonger wasp hovered in the air, sucking blood from the fox carcass through its long proboscis. Harry's eyes were glued to the macabre scene for several seconds.

He tip-toed back to Juno, took her hand and led her to view the hideous goings on. Eventually, after dragging her away without speaking, they passed through a gap in the thick hedge around the wood, where he suddenly snapped, "Run," and they legged it down the lane.

"What was that weird clicking noise?" asked Juno, tripping over her own feet as she tried to keep up. Without answering, Harry stretched his legs and ran even harder until, finally reaching the confines of Juno's garden, where both of them dropped heavily onto seats. Holding his sides, he panted and stared at the floor while answering.

"The noise came from the Deathmonger's

mandibles, clicking together as it carved chunks of raw flesh from the fox... And the other bones nearby suggest that that monster wasp has been active in the area for some time." Juno looked shocked and began rubbing both hands up and down her legs nervously.

"Did you only see one of them?" she asked.

"I think so," said Harry, raising his head slowly to meet the nervous stare of Juno as she prepared to speak.

"We must tell Mum. She's the only one who will believe us. I'm scared. Scared for us and scared that Mum will be left to sort out this mess on her own."

"Don't worry," answered Harry supportively. "If those idiotic scientists won't help, I will." He placed one hand on Juno's shoulder and continued. "I've had years of experience fighting wasps. Not giant ones, of course, but the principle's the same."

Juno smiled, unexpectedly gripping her earlobe between finger and thumb before speaking randomly. "Hi Mum, sorry to trouble you at the lab, but we've found out something vital. Do you remember the boy who passed by the house yesterday? Yes, the one with the old bicycle..." Juno stopped speaking, suddenly, and mouthed an apology to Harry. She reached over, placed the palm of one hand onto the right side of his head, then continued to tell her mother of the wasp sighting. Harry flinched as the unspoken words of an unknown woman echoed inside his skull and Juno responded, verbally... "No, we didn't see how it escaped, Mum, no."

"I knew it. This is a catastrophe," came the inner voice, "We must discover how that Deathmonger wasp got out and whether it returned to the compound to pass on the information. I'll report to Dr Shizzle right away. Let's hope he takes me seriously this time. Thanks for the alert. I'll speak to you later, darling. Take care."

"See you later, Mum," replied Juno, "Oh, we might pop over to the museum on the solar tube this afternoon but, bye for now." Releasing her ear and removing the palm of her hand from Harry's head, she noticed the startled expression on his face.

"That was my mother... Transmitting by neuro-implant," she clarified. "Whenever I pinch my ear and think of her, the call goes out. The other person needs an implant, too, of course, but the signal will travel through the palm of my hand; that's how you heard part of the conversation. I take it no one in your family has a chipcom device, then?" Juno chuckled. "Anyway, do you fancy that trip into town? We could look at the old cars in the museum, like I said earlier? You'll probably be a tad more clued up about those than you are on the latest communication systems. The tube station is less than a mile away."

"Sure," said Harry, and the two of them strode off in the opposite direction to the spinney.

Ambling through the long grass, a short while later, a stunningly diverse range of animals could be seen wandering about in full view. Sheep, cows, horses, rabbits, goats and hares all grazed the same rich pastures, while up above, buzzards and red kites circled, waiting for an opportunity to pick off their abundant prey. Soon, several fallow deer came into view, pulling berries from low hanging tree branches whilst hogs snuffled in the hedge bottoms. Beyond this, a gigantic, caterpillar-like structure snaked away into the distance. The route of the tube line was punctuated by battery crane towers in both directions.

"I dare say you've never travelled by solar vacuum tube before, what, with having a bicycle to ride... Do you even know how they work?" teased Juno, walking into the station and pinching her ear again. "Trantham museum, please," she said, and almost immediately, two pairs of sliding doors opened, allowing access through an outer tube to the train inside. Feeling slightly panicked, Harry launched himself on board and sat down hastily to hear an automated voice ringing out.

"All passengers, please fasten your seat belts? Stops by mental request only." As the tube whisked away, the trees merged into a green blur, barely visible through the opaque walls of the tube, and Harry turned to Juno, trying to sound calm.

"Actually, I have been on the tube before, and I do know how they work. The SVT is a vacuum aided rapid transit system, running on solar energy with battery-crane backup. The outer skin is constructed from semi-rigid, solar sensitive, reinforced fabric. The battery units are made by Solabat, a world leader in chemical-free, power storage systems." Harry looked pleased with himself and expected Juno to be equally impressed.

"Spot on. Almost word for word what it says on the information board back at the station. Funny, that." Juno laughed, un-clipping her seatbelt and pinching her ear, while Harry leapt to his feet. Seconds later, the train cruised to a standstill. "Trantham station. All visitors, please disembark promptly. Thank you for travelling by SVT."

"Solar-Vacuum-tube. Nice bit of kit," said Harry, under his breath, stepping out of the train onto a slow-moving travelator. After following a curved tunnel, to arrive at the nearby museum, a shiny car, just inside the door, caught his eye, and he struggled to hide his amazement.

"My ...... A Ford Anglia," he corrected, skipping around the car gleefully. "With perfect front wings and normal headlamps." Juno, registering his high spirits, chuckled then addressed him.

"I thought you'd be in your element here. And what a coincidence you're interested in Ford Anglias." Harry ignored the remark, opened the driver's door and climbed in, winding down the window enthusiastically and wiggling the steering wheel for the first time in one hundred years. Meanwhile, Juno explained what she meant.

"This car was discovered by my grandfather at the back of a barn thirty years ago. All covered in pigeon droppings, it had no front wings and a hole in the roof, can you believe? The headlamps were stuffed inside old paint tins riveted to the bonnet. I know, it sounds bonkers. Grandpa spent two years on a full restoration before donating the car to the museum." Harry flushed bright red, saying nothing until, as they left the museum, he pointed to a familiar building.

"Is there a supermarket in the shopping centre over there? We're out of porridge at the campsite, and I fancy some strawberry jelly, too."

"Shopping centre?... Supermarket?" said Juno, "There you go, living in the past again." She pinched her ear twice in quick succession and laughed out loud. "Porridge oats and jelly sorted. Your items will be ready for collection at the SVT station when we get back, my treat. Now let's go and eat ice cream."

After trailing through a pedestrian area, dotted with neatly presented flower beds, trees with wrap around benches, Cafes and restaurants, they were soon eating from a single large bowl of ice cream, using two spoons.

"I'll pay for this; how much is it?" asked Harry.

"Sixty-five pounds, but it's okay, Mum insisted

it's her treat," replied Juno. "And right now, thanks to you, she's busy working out how the compound fences could have been breached. Apparently, Shizzle is still in denial, so the task is proving rather difficult.

"What's your mother's name," asked Harry.

"Stella," answered Juno, "And I think she likes you because you've been invited for tea tomorrow?"

Harry coughed in embarrassment. "That'd be nice," he said, scraping his chair against the tiled floor as the two friends got up and set off back to the SVT. After disembarking from the tube, Juno stepped over to a covered area and picked up a package. "There you go. Porridge for breakfast with jelly for afters." Harry laughed and thanked her graciously before escorting her home with a promise to call the following day.

Marching up the road, a veil of fear descended as he passed the copse nervously, eyes peeled and ears pinned back. Thankfully, though, there was nothing unusual to see or hear. Upon reaching the air raid shelters, the more familiar rasping sound of Lou on her trail bike met Harry's ears. She accelerated aggressively towards him and pulled a massive wheelie. After skidding to a halt, cutting the engine and performing a drum roll on the petrol tank, she slouched back on the seat and flashed her white teeth cheekily.

"How's darling Juno today? It must be true love; you were gone for ages, AGAIN."

"Haha, very funny, but you'll never believe what I saw in town," replied Harry, enthusiastically... Lou shrugged.

"Rivet. He is on display in the museum in fully restored, pristine condition."

"Don't talk wet," said Lou. "That car was falling to bits in 1979. It has to be dust by now. There's more than one Ford Anglia in the world, you know."

"Yeah, but this was the exact same colour and everything."

"Big deal, cloth brain. What were you doing in a museum anyway? We're supposed to be keeping a low profile."

Harry changed tack suddenly.

"Never mind that. While I was out, I nearly got stung by a giant, escaped wasp. I think it was one of a nasty new breed of monster Deathmongers. Apparently, they've been genetically modified. Capable of paralysing small animals or birds with one sting. That's animals we're talking about, not just insects! Juno's mum's boss swears it can't have come from the compound, but I'm certain it did. I'm wondering how many more are already the wrong side of the fence?"

"Deathmonger wasp... Did you say Death-monger? Well, that name says it all." Lou looked decidedly rattled. "I think it's time we got off back to 1979 where the wasps are a normal-size. I'm allergic to the thought of flesh melting stings or being paralysed, not to mention, wasps sucking my blood and their wriggling larvae eating me alive. Any of those things would upset me just as much as it would the course of history, and Dad warned us not to do that. He and Mum are due back any minute; we should see what they think."

Literally, as she spoke, their two red-faced parents pulled up on the bicycles, dismounted and leaned their steeds on either side of a tree.

"Phew," said Mrs S, "That hill's a killer. I had to push my bike most of the way."
"The hill's not the only killer around here," muttered Lou, just loud enough for her parents to hear.

"What do you mean, Louise?" asked John, eyeballing his daughter, suspiciously.
Lou was about to explain when Harry interrupted, desperate to avoid revealing the Deathmonger situation. He was worried his mother might ban them from staying on and he had no intention of abandoning either Juno or Stella. Rolling his eyes in Lou's direction, he quickly changed the subject.

"We can't wait to see the look on Stan's face when he and Bill unearth that empty sandwich box tomorrow, can we Lou? And, don't forget, I'd like to borrow your camera, Dad, to capture the action, if I may?" After an uncomfortable silence,

Lou, realising that her macho image was at stake, backed up her brother with a sheepish nod and defused the situation.

"I was talking about all of those killer wasps INSIDE the compound, Dad. But there's no cause for alarm with them all being secure." She snarled in her brother's direction, then continued. "In fact, now that my trail bike has been rescued and with the ruby safe, I'm happy as Larry. In fact, I've never been happier." Lou issued a fake laugh, and sensing his sister's underlying angst, Harry decided to offer her the opportunity to escape from danger.

"Actually, Lou and me have had a difference of opinion over whether it's worth staying to watch Bill and Stan, tomorrow, AND we argued about who'd take the photos if we did. So, I think Lou should travel home with you, then she can bring back her own camera if she decides to return in the morning. We could each drive a separate vehicle home tomorrow night and put the bikes in the car boot to avoid upsetting history by leaving them behind. There'd be no problem caused, what ever Lou decides to do." Harry looked directly at his mother and threw in a final tempter. "Of course, if you fancy the thrill of riding shotgun behind Dad on the motorbike tonight, instead of going in the car, Lou'll have to stop here and share the camera with me."

The thought of avoiding a sixty-five miles per hour jaunt, clinging to her husband's waist, whilst perched on a small leather seat, settled it. Their mother agreed without argument, but Lou suddenly felt affronted. Had she just been cut out of the action? Her brother seemed extremely keen for her not to return. Perhaps his Deathmonger story was all a total lie? A mere plot, so that Harry could spend more time with Juno? Lou decided to call her brother's bluff. She would depart, but only for the one night. Leaving him alone would teach him a lesson. Harry'd be petrified in the shelter alone, and as a result, he might finally start appreciating her, huh.

"It's a simple fact, I'd get better photos with my own camera," she agreed. "Therefore, Harry's quick jaunt home idea is a good one." The matter was resolved and Mrs Scrambles re-assumed her usual, bossy manner.

"Right, let's get the car packed and light a fire. There's time for a bite to eat before the Corridor of Light forms."

With the demolition of a corned beef hash leaving them all in a buoyant mood, John related details of the motorbike rescue and made a final address to his son.
"So, what about the ruby then, Harry? How do we return it to the proper authorities?"

"Isn't that obvious?" muscled in Lou. "Harry plans to leave it for darling Juno to hand over. I only hope we can trust her not to flog it on the black market." She looked scornfully at Harry, waiting for the inevitable defence of his new friend, which followed immediately.

"Juno solved the cryptic clue, so she deserves the reward anyway. And I trust her completely. With the original map to provide a credible excuse for discovering the ruby, neither Bill, Stan, nor the authorities will be any the wiser over our involvement."

"Here, here," said Mrs Scrambles. "Juno sounds like a lovely girl to me." Lou scowled in irritation as the entire family stood up to say their goodbyes, and a few minutes later, Rivet sped past Harry with his sister at the wheel. With a powerful downdraught pushing over the grass stems and wild flowers, the car entered the Corridor of Light, its gleaming bumpers sending shafts of light dancing in all directions. Then, in a flash, Harry found himself alone.

Turning slowly, he focused on the rabbits, hopping across the glade and watched pigeons swooping from the sky to roost in the tree canopy. After a while, breaking off a long stem of Cocksfoot grass to chew like his grandpa would have done, he began wondering about what Bert must have thought upon arrival in 1843. Queen Victoria was on the throne and Charles Dickens would have been busy writing 'A Christmas Carol'. Harry had also read that the world's first Christmas cards were sent in that year. Being a farmer, Bert would probably have found work quickly in rural

Lincolnshire and might even have settled down to start a new family... Perhaps them searching for him was a bad idea. A startling thought suddenly struck Harry like a thunderbolt. What if Grandpa Bert didn't want to return home at all?

Harry's mind returned to 2079, and, sauntering into the shelter, he stoked the fire, then sat down on a tin can. Reaching into his pocket, he popped a piece of bubble gum into his mouth, working the pink blob until a giant balloon formed. The bubble burst messily against his face, and whilst retrieving sweet fragments with his tongue, he raised his feet to warm them against the fire. Then blew an even bigger gum ball.

With that, a loud, monotone buzz, suddenly, dropped into earshot, echoing down the shelter from the opposite end. Something was hovering by the entrance.

Harry grabbed a burning stick from the fire and fumbled for a torch with his other hand. Goosebumps sprang up all over his body, then globules of sweat appeared like drops of rain on a car windscreen. His arm hairs stood rigidly on end as a relentless shiver ran down his spine at the familiar sound of clicking. The noise got rapidly louder, and gently laying the torch on a nearby drum, Harry sent a beam of light flashing along the bunker. With a pumping heart, he gripped the burning stick tightly in both hands and held his breath. A stretched shadow appeared on the curved white concrete wall, then the insect's head and pulsating abdomen hovered into full view. Two compound eyes glistened in the torchlight as the giant wasp scanned the bunker, its antennae wriggling like spider's legs. Harry was petrified and mesmerised in equal measure.

"Deathmonger or hornet?" he whispered, his heart rising into his mouth. One thing was clear, this wasp was a queen, looking for somewhere to build a nest, and he was trapped in a dead-end tunnel! Harry's legs began to shake uncontrollably and then the unthinkable happened. Without warning the gum bubble burst, plastering his face with a sticky sweet mess.

The insect's antennae reacted instantly. Hundreds of microscopic sensors homed in on the sweet odour as the flying fortress buzzed towards the sugary food source. At that point Harry was sure his heart had stopped beating entirely and large beads of sweat rolled freely down his face, dripping off his chin to sizzle against the red embers of the burning stick. Feeling dizzy and ready to collapse to the floor at the mercy of the wasp, he anticipating the excruciating agony of multiple vicious stings. This would be followed by swiftly spreading paralysis, then violent dissection whilst he was still alive and fully concious. Harry went white in the face. It seemed a living hell was certain to be followed by an even more grizzly death.

The buzzing predator edged slowly closer, but then a wisp of smoke drifted from the burning stick to cross both antennae. The huge wasp flinched, turning momentarily sideways to display the warning colours of its throbbing, venom-filled abdomen and gleaming needlepoint sting. Harry's fate hung in the balance. Then, mercifully, a larger curl of smoke mixed with his own vaporized sweat, wafted down the shelter, upsetting the insect's sensitivity. It moved away slowly, eventually, disappearing outside.

Harry banged his chest with the side of a fist to restart his heart, peeled the sticky gum from his face and threw it into the fire with disgust. The gum flared up as the remaining sugar burnt off, and he tried to stand up, but neither leg would work. After massaging both thighs for several minutes, he made a second attempt. This time his tired lower limbs responded and picking up the torch from the drum, he hobbled to the entrance with the smouldering stick acting as a crutch.

A glimmer of daylight remained and after peeping around the end wall of the bunker, he ducked back inside. The predatory beast still hovered less than ten metres away. Plucking up the courage for another look, he watched the wasp disappear into the next bunker along. "Otto," he said, out loud. "Looks like I'm gonna be living next door to Alice... A giant wasp. That's not what the doctor ordered, at all."

Back inside his shelter, he draped Lou's sleeping bag across the doorway, pinning it in place with loose bricks, and retreated to the fire. After adding several logs, enough to keep it going through the night, he zipped himself up to the neck in his sleeping bag, laid back, then fell into a fitful sleep.

After awaking, with a start, from a dream in which he was cocooned by a giant spider and about to be stung by giant wasps, Harry performed a Houdini stunt on his sleeping bag and quickly made up the fire. It was dawn. Lou would be here soon and for once he was looking forward to seeing her. A cautious reccy outside revealed no sign of insects and he relaxed slightly. The cheerful dawn chorus rang out, with Robins and Wrens accompanied by chattering Magpies. Feeling happier, he ventured further afield, savouring the fresh scent of wet grass and tree fungus. WET GRASS? A state of panic dropped like a heavy dark cloak to suffocate him. It was raining. This meant Lou might not be back after all. The possibility had not previously crossed his mind. He imagined himself alone, living next door to Alice, like in the song. Except, in the song, Alice was a girl, not a dangerous giant wasp! He hesitated, then laughed to himself. Somehow, naming the predatory queen had made her less scary. He would hang onto that title.

As the rain came on more heavily, he ducked back inside the bunker. At least Alice would be confined to her shelter, too. Heating up some slightly iffy milk to make a large bowl of porridge, he pulled the bag of sherbet pips from his pocket and sprinkled a generous handful on top. Harry watched as they sank below the milky layer, then five minutes later, licking out the bowl to save on the washing up, he rocked back on his tin drum, feeling much better. The rain had stopped, allowing him to venture outside and over to the edge of the crop compound.

Here the sun already shone. Bright light illuminated the tiger striped abdomens of several wasps, already out and about, and Harry noticed two distinct sizes. A larger one swooped down right in front of him. This, he assumed was a Deathmonger, identical to the one seen the day before, and twice the size of Alice. The wasp started digging and soon disappeared from sight, its mandibles clicking in time with tiny granules of earth which spewed backwards from the hole. Then, after a few more seconds, the wasp reappeared and began furiously cleaning mud from its mandibles. Despite rubbing them together forcefully, the sticky dirt wasn't shifting. Eventually, the insect scuttled over to a puddle, dipped its entire head into the water, and resumed the cleaning process until all traces of soil were gone. Following the strange ritual, the deadly Deathmonger sunned itself for several minutes, then flew off.

Harry hurried away, making a beeline for the shelter, whilst consumed with a single thought. What were the Deathmongers burying? This was the second time he had caught one digging a hole. Arriving at the Orthostats, he consulted his watch, it read 7.15 AM. The sun had risen while he was away but there was no sign of Lou. Perhaps it was still cloudy in 1979, thought Harry. Batting the negative thoughts away, he considered his next move. Juno might want to go with him to Felton Hall? Yes, that was it. Suddenly feeling more positive, he rummaged for his father's camera, rushed to the trail bike and soon found himself outside her little wooden house.

Perching on the motorcycle seat for some while, he watched the crane shifting blocks majestically behind the house until eventually, Juno emerged from inside and ran across to greet him. The strong sunlight set the chrome motorbike wheels glistening, and she swooned around the machine.

"Wow, this is so great. And rare, too. Where did you get it?" Harry dropped the side-stand and got off.

"It's been passed down through the family. I only get to use it on special occasions, and today is definitely one of those."

"Really? Is it your Birthday?"

"No. It's the day Bill and Stan get to dig up an empty sandwich box in the middle of a media frenzy," Harry chortled. Juno gleamed back in astonishment just as a set of sliding glass doors opened at the front of the house and a middle-aged woman stepped into the garden. The lady walked over, smiling broadly.

"Hello, I'm Stella, Juno's mother. Very pleased to meet you at last." Harry offered his hand, feeling slightly awkward, and she shook it firmly. Soon, with home made tea and biscuits served, they engaged in conversation.

"I worked all through last night, trying to persuade Dr Shizzle what a horribly dangerous critter the Deathmonger wasp is, but the man's a complete twerp. He sees his creation through rose-tinted spectacles and won't listen to a word I say." She paused to take on a defiant look. "Nevertheless, one way or another, we will find out how those wasps are escaping." Harry nodded calmly and answered.

"Has anyone considered the possibility that Deathmongers have learned to tunnel beneath the fences? The drones in the buffer zone would not detect them underground, and the fences would have little or no effect." Stella clutched Harry's arm tightly.

"Of course... And why not. Many species of wasp build their nests underground. How did we not foresee that they might dig their way out? A tunnel would allow easy return trips to the compound, which means details of how to escape may already have been passed to other wasps," she exclaimed. " Thousands of new queens are about to be dispatched to compounds worldwide, possibly armed with this information. My God." Juno sprang to her feet and took hold of her mother's shaking hands.

"There's no time to be lost, mum. We must pace the entire perimeter, find the tunnels and block them in the hope that we are not to late." Stella nodded and dispatched Juno to fetch spades from the garden shed, while Harry yelled after her.

"We'll need watering cans, too. Wet soil clags their mandibles. Dousing the ground should stop the Deathmongers re-digging their tunnels while we think of a plan B."

Stella disappeared indoors, soon returning with several syringes of anti-venom, just in case, and they set off hurriedly down the lane. Along the way, Harry continued to garble in nervous excitement. "The fact that it rained overnight will help prevent new tunnels from being dug, for now, But we must come up with a long term plan to stop the Deathmongers altogether. The entire world is in serious jeopardy."

Arriving at the perimeter of the compound, they split into two groups. Harry headed towards the shelters with a spade and one watering can; While Juno and Stella set off the other way around.

"Let's aim to meet halfway in about forty-five

minutes," bawled Harry over his shoulder before, five minutes later, he found the first tunnel. Being predictably close to the copse at the end of Juno's lane, it was the size of a mouse hole. Harry shovelled three spades of dirt into the opening, tamped down the soil and watered the surrounding area before continuing around the perimeter fence. Scanning the ground as he went, he soon reached the air raid shelters.

This was the moment of truth for Alice. A tunnel in the vicinity would raise the possibility that she, too, was a Deathmonger. No tunnel would point to her being a mere hornet queen. Harry had developed a strange attachment to Alice and had no wish to see her dead.

Relieved to find no sign of Deathmonger escape holes nearby, a sudden loud buzz sent him ducking for cover as Alice swooped by. Recognising the hornet, he relaxed, edging closer to watch the graceful queen chewing decayed wood from a fallen tree and forming it into a bolus with her mandibles. Close up, it was clear that Alice's wings were more orangey than the wasps inside the compound. He imagined the regal hornet, busily sculpting perfect hexagonal cells in which to lay her eggs. The dedication and hard work required to build such an amazing nest left him in awe. A moment later, Alice flew off, leaving Harry suddenly conscious of the time. Not wishing to miss the Ginger Cake media show, he checked his watch and was relieved to find it was only eleven. There was still plenty of time to get to Felton Hall, and, just then, he spotted Stella with Juno heading towards him.

"Any luck?" he shouted ahead. "I found one escape route, but that's all. What about you?"

"None at all-round our side, thank goodness. With a bit of luck, only a single wasp has escaped so far, and hopefully not an egg laying queen."

When they all met up, Stella continued by heaping praise on Harry for his quick thinking.

"Your thought of wetting the soil to clag their mandibles was a great idea," she said enthusiastically, but her supportive smile quickly degenerated into a look of concern.

"My worry is that if a single Deathmonger, has passed on escape details, other wasps will begin to dig out in their thousands. We must convince Shizzle of the threat, then work with him to find a solution, though Lord knows what we can do about the situation at this stage."

Harry suddenly felt as though a mosquito was flitting around his brain, tickling different portions as he desperately searched for inspiration. The Deathmonger species had to be wiped from the face of the earth. The question was, how? The utopian world had long since given up dangerous pesticides, ironically developing the Deathmonger wasp to fulfil that very role. Now, the wasps were on the verge of colonising the planet and there was no quick fix, no supply of chemicals to halt their spread. He closed his eyes, breathed in a lung full of fresh spring air, then opened them to face the pair of bright blue sparkles belonging to Juno. Here before him stood his great great granddaughter, and her intense stare filled him with renewed confidence.

"I know you'll find a way to help us, Harry; I just know it. Lateral thinking, that's where the answer lies... Just like with the cryptic clue on the ruby map. It's a simple matter of applying your mind."

Energised by Juno's remarks, Harry felt on the verge of a breakthrough, with the tiniest of brainwaves humming inside his head, about to crystallise. Hoping a change of subject might clear the blockage, he moved on.

"I'm sure we'll sort out the Deathmonger threat soon enough, but in the meantime, we've a pantomime to watch. This afternoon's stars of the show, will be Stan and Bill, supposedly unearthing the missing ruby. I wondered... Would you be interested in coming along to watch?"

Juno nodded eagerly and after explaining the ruby saga to her mother, Harry made an unexpected request of Stella.

"Your daughter helped me decipher the map, so I would like her to be the one handing the ruby to the authorities when all of this is over. Will you store the ruby safely here until then?" he said, pulling both the jewel and the map from his pocket, pressing them into Juno's palm and squeezing her hand closed. Juno unfolded her fingers slowly, to stare at the ruby.

"Wow, it's so beautiful. Are you sure you want me to do this, Harry? Why don't we do it together?"

"Nah... Publicity makes me nervous," he said quickly. "I'd rather you did it without me."

"Well, in that case, I'd love to. Perhaps Mum could come along, too?" Harry nodded before answering.

"That settles it then, but I'd prefer not to be mentioned at all, I just don't feel comfortable being in the public eye." He smiled at Stella who took the gem from her daughter, stored it safely indoors, and no more was said on the subject.

CHAPTER 8. HOW TO CATCH A DEATHMONGER

Two hours later, Harry steered the trail bike into a field on the outskirts of Felton village, dismounted and then disguised the machine with bracken. This done, he and Juno set off across country to the icehouse, about a mile away, where they spotted a distant group of people gathered outside the stately home. With no one yet at the Mirror pond, it was simply a case of climbing the tree-covered grassy mound above the icehouse. Once in position they had a clear view of the entire ruby burial site.

"I can't wait for Stan and Bill to get the celebrity treatment they've craved," said Harry, rubbing his hands together and lying down on his stomach next to Juno. Soon, the distant procession set off at a ceremonial pace along a gravel footpath towards the Mirror pond, and he made ready with the camera. Several media technicians could be seen shuffling backwards in front of the parade, fighting to record every step made by the two celebrities.

Stan was dressed more smartly than Harry had ever seen him, and Bill looked equally dapper. Both crooks were clean-shaven with slicked-back hair. Stan guided the group to the North West corner of the Mirror pond, where Bill held the map aloft for the benefit of the paparazzi. At the same time, Juno sniggered as she whispered across to Harry.

"This is such fun. Those men look so smarmy, I can see how they could easily be dishonest." Harry nodded and smiled inwardly at the thought of what was to come. All of a sudden, a silence fell over the crowd and the procession came to a standstill.

Stan began to talk, with the reporters lapping up his every word until Bill shoved his friend impatiently aside, adding to the speech in a posh voice.

"Since we discovered the ruby map, hidden inside an ancient marmalade jar, Stanley and I have worked relentlessly to solve the cryptic clue. Finally, we succeeded. As a result, the gem is about to be discovered and reinstated as rightful centrepiece of the Imperial State Crown after an absence of one hundred years. Many thanks to each and every one of you for attending today. Please enjoy this truly historic moment of national pride."

"Here here," muttered Harry as the crowd began a slow chant.

"Ruby, ruby, ruby..." After bathing in the glory for a moment, Stan held up his hand regally, and the people fell silent.

"Following our interpretation of the cryptic clue, we believe the word fridge refers to the old icehouse, just over there." He pointed into the distance as the crowd collectively drew breath. "The fridge maker must therefore be the Mirror Pond from which ice was skimmed to stock the icehouse. That pond has a distinct North-West corner which is the point from where we will now follow the further directions on the map."

The murmuring crowd nodded their approval and fell into a hush as Stan moved into position at the North West corner of the Mirror Pond and raised his voice further.

"Read out those directions please, Bill." His words were accompanied by enthusiastic applause.

"First, Stanley, it says face North East," said Bill.

Stan withdrew a compass from his pocket, tapped it, then rotated his body...

"Now: Forward 32 strides..." began Bill, before continuing line by line, after allowing Stan to follow each instruction. "Left 6... forward 17... Right 21... Forward 11... Right 2... Back 6...

The crowd indulged in several sharp intakes of breath until finally, Bill raised his hand to regain public control. After a moment's silence, he continued to explain the rest of the directions on the map.

"The next line comprises fourteen dashes which we conclude, each relate to the measurement of an average sized man's foot," he said. "Therefore, Stanley... Sideways fourteen feet and forward thirteen feet."

Stan made ready to pivot on his heels, but at that moment a voice in the crowd shouted, "Sideways?.... But, do you mean left or right?" A horrified gasp echoed over the Mirror Pond, and Stan appeared shocked into silence before bursting into cackling laughter.

"Left or right indeed?" he prattled as the reporters swerved their microphones closer to his face.

"Sounds like a red herring to me," whispered Juno, up on the mound, and before Harry could answer, Stan confirmed the fact, speaking in his usual nasal twang.

"As the sideways instruction lacks a directional clause, we believe it should be ignored. It is a clear red herring." The crowd began speculating amongst themselves, but Stan silenced them quickly. "Please be patient, for in a moment we shall know the truth," he said, and the people nodded enthusiastically.

"The final instructions read as follows:

FORWARD THIRTEEN FEET," said Bill. Stan began placing one foot in front of another, while the crowd joined in for the final count down.

"Seven, six, five, four, three, two, one, Jackpot!"

Stan froze and pulled a slender stick with a Union Jack flag at one end from his tunic, prodding it into the ground. After folding the map, Bill reached for a fork and two camera-clad journalists clambered up hastily provided stepladders to acquire prime photography spots. The rest of the crowd formed a tight circle.

Digging tentatively around the pea-stick, a dull thud soon rang out, at which point Stan rolled his eyes at the crowd and dropped to his knees. He pulled out a small trowel and began scraping away the soil like a professional archaeologist until the Tupperware box came into view. He stopped digging and raised the box carefully, before placing it onto a velvet topped pedestal that had been hastily positioned by officials. After donning a pair of silk gloves, Stan peeled back the tough plastic lid amid total silence from the audience. Reaching inside the box, he triumphantly lifted the gleaming ruby high into the air, while up on the hill, Juno raised her head in shock.

"What's going on? I thought the ruby was at my house." Harry grinned and pointed back to the plinth where Stan appeared to be sniffing the ruby. An initial bemused look suddenly exploded into one of nauseating horror. Something was seriously wrong, but the crowd had no clue what.

All at once, Stan hurled the ruby in a violent fashion at the trunk of a nearby tree, where it shattered into a thousand pieces.

Gasps were followed by momentary silence and then a full-scale riot broke out with ordinary men and women grappling excitedly over each and every particle. The cameras rolled-on as the crowd's exuberance suddenly turned to anger.

"This ruby is nothing but strawberry jelly," yelled a stout man, hurling his blob at a slim lady who reciprocated with full force. Another man, dramatically chewed, then swallowed a sizeable red lump, right in front of a video camera as the mad jelly fight spread quickly around him.

Harry's face, meanwhile, was glowing with utter contentment and he turned to Juno.

"I made a replica ruby from the strawberry jelly you bought the other day. It seemed only fair that the jewel thieves' descendants received a suitable booby prize for their efforts."

Juno chuckled, adjusting her focus back to the angry hoard, desperate to vent their fury on Stan and Bill who were mere flitting specks in the distance. As the crowd ran off in pursuit, Harry summed up the event.

"I doubt the Ginger Cake Gang will earn a free lifetimes membership of the National Thrust, after their performance today," he said, and rising to their feet, he and Juno strode gleefully away.

Back at the cottage, Stella was waiting in the garden. After making a fresh pot of tea, she listened patiently to Juno and Harry describing the pantomime performance. Eventually, Stella moved the conversation on to a more dangerous topic. "While you've been gone, I've spoken to Dr Shizzle. He informed me that no action would be taken without direct evidence that at least one Deathmonger wasp has actually escaped. We need to catch a specimen to prove our story. Only then will he agree to a wasp cull, which must occur in an ecologically sound way, in strict accordance with current laws." There was a long pause as Harry took in Stella's words and considered them carefully before responding.

"Catching a Deathmonger will be hard, but we can do it, I'm sure."

"Catch a Deathmonger? Catch a Deathmonger...? Came a high-pitched voice from bushes at the edge of the garden. "Are you away with the fairies?"

With everyone looking up, Lou stepped into view, storming across the lawn to continue her spiel. "A good old fashioned dose of insecticide is what those wasps need. Wipe out the lot of 'em, Never mind catching one. We're talking apex predators here. Top killers. Destroy them before they destroy us, that's what I say." She pushed her way past Juno and Stella, directing a further onslaught at Harry.

"And, where were you this morning? Not waiting by the Corri...er, I mean, "Not waiting by the Corner of the woods as we agreed... But don't worry, I made my own way to Felton Hall and credit where credit's due, Harry, replacing the ruby with a strawberry jelly replica was a master stroke. I got some great photos." She softened her stance, smirked at her brother, then turned to face Juno and Stella, who were standing wide-eyed in amazement at the vocal power of this short-haired girl whom they'd never met.

"May I introduce my charming sister, Louise," said Harry with a loud chuckle. Stella and Juno shook hands with Lou, but after exchanging pleasantries, Stella was keen to put Lou right on several points.

"I'm surprised at your level of aggression towards these insects, Louise," she said. "Don't you know, wasps form a valuable part of the ecosystem in dealing with pests? Everyone agrees, insecticides were banned for the good of the planet. It seems you've been reading too many old comic books my girl. May I politely suggest that it is you who is, 'away with the fairies." Lou shrank back in shock, but at that moment Harry leapt to his feet.

"Away with the fairies... The fairies. That's it...That's the answer... That's how we can ethically remove the Deathmonger species from the face of the earth. By using fairy flies."

"Eh?" Both Lou and Juno screwed up their faces in unison while Harry shook his fist and rattled on excitedly.

"It'll be the ultimate David and Goliath story... Fairy flies are the world's smallest insect, I read about them in my wasp book. Actually, not flies at all, but tiny parasitoid wasps, barely visible under the microscope. Nevertheless, they are capable of exploiting the one weak spot of their giant predatory cousin."

With Lou, spiralling into a new state of fury, she gesticulated frantically at Harry.
"Weak spot. What weak spot? The Deathmongers have no weak spot. The clue's in the name... Deathmonger and the words, monstrous apex predator. These are the world's ultimate killers. What chance will the planet's smallest insect have against such a mighty wasp? and what does parasitoid mean anyway?" Harry's reply came in a quiet voice.

"Parasitoids feed on the larvae of other insects, bringing about their gradual demise. And the Deathmonger can't destroy what they can't see, so the fairy flies will be like undercover agents. They'll invade the Deathmonger nests and kill the larvae ethically, in accordance with all of nature's rules."

"But, how will such a tiny insect get near the Deathmonger nests in the first place?" asked Lou, quickly. Harry paused.

"It'll be tricky, but that's where we come in," he said. "We must position the fairy flies close by each and every individual nest so they can crawl inside and lay their eggs... Fortunately for us, adult fairy flies have an aquatic phase, so the water vessels below each Deathmonger nest are the answer. If we can place them inside the tanks, the fairy flies will achieve extinction by stealth. The perfect answer."

"I see what you're saying," enthused Stella. "We already have a small stock of fairy flies in the lab, normally used for the biological control of red spider mite. I see no reason why they wouldn't attack the wasp larvae if we can get sufficient numbers into the nests."

"Wow," said Juno, "Who'd have thought it, eh? The Deathmonger, not an apex predator, after all. Toppled by the tiniest insect in the world. Amazing. But let's not forget, we have to capture an escaped Deathmonger first. Shizzle needs to believe us before he will authorise their destruction."After Juno's final words, Lou sat down heavily and went through several shades of pale.

"But, why can't we just kill this one specimen wasp the easy way?" she begged. "We've no need to tell anyone... A single Deathmonger would be enough to persuade this Chizzle fellow... dead OR alive, right?"

"What a shocking suggestion," scolded Stella,

"Killing a wasp is against our constitutional law. No individual should ever set out to end the life of another living thing. The Deathmonger must be caught alive, unless we find one that has met with a natural end." Lou's shoulders fell in acceptance of Stella's words; then, after a moment of contemplation, she stood up, looking focused and determined.

"Okay. Let's go catch us a monster wasp, then. But we need a proper plan... A Lou plan, for once." Lou quickly aired her idea and with no one able to come up with anything better, Stella disappeared into the house. She reappeared with a large butterfly net, a thick cotton pillowcase, and four syringes of anti-venom in case of disaster. Thus equipped, the team set off on their critical mission.

At the spinney, Harry peered cautiously around a large tree trunk, where a rabbit grazed happily on the juicy sward a few feet away. After several minutes, the monstrous Deathmonger wasp swooped out of nowhere, buzzing loudly. The evil creature latched onto the sizeable animal with both mandibles, inflicting a powerful sting which sent the rabbit into immediate spasm. As the lethal predator concentrated on dissecting its prey, Harry stepped out from behind the tree and sneaked closer with his butterfly net raised. Lowering it gently with one hand, he beckoned Lou with the other.

"How we are going to get the wasp into the bag?"

she whispered. "It might realise what's happening, and when you try and lift the net, it could fly out."

"Get nearer with the pillowcase wide open, and I'll swerve the net inside in one swift movement," hissed Harry.

Lou edged forwards, but confirming her worst fear, the wasp suddenly turned and finding itself trapped, reared onto its hind legs. A familiar clicking sound signalled the worst of intentions, and a terrified Harry screamed loudly.

"It's cutting through the net!"

With a first slit already visible, the Deathmonger rapidly carved the hole wider as Lou dropped the pillowcase, limply.

"Run," she shrieked, dashing through the bushes after Stella and Juno, but it was too late for Harry. The net burst wide apart, and five evil eyes drilled into him. A split second later, the Deathmonger launched itself.

Harry was frozen with fear and a moment away from a gruesome death. Lowering his head and about to close his eyes in submission, he suddenly caught sight of a set of dagger-like claws, appearing between his knees. There was a high-pitched yowl and a furry limb side-swiped the Deathmonger's head, killing it instantly. The monster wasp crash-landed heavily, and Harry released the handle of the tattered net, watching as it fell slowly to the ground beside the monstrous, dead Deathmonger.

A soft brushing sensation against his leg was followed by a purring meow, which reawakened Harry's senses.

"Dirtbag?" he exclaimed.

Having heard the feline-rumpus, the others stopped mid-flight, turned and then approached cautiously with Lou adding to her brother's words of surprise.

"Dirtbag, you crafty thing. Secretly following us all this time?"

"Thank goodness he did," said Harry. "We'd be goners otherwise; that wasp was pure evil. It'd've paralysed the lot of us before anyone could've applied anti-venom."

Stella and Juno looked down at the lifeless Deathmonger wasp with sorrowful expressions. "Poor thing," they said simultaneously.

"Poor thing, poor thing," shouted Lou. "Should've sprayed it off like I said. Lucky to be alive, we are."

"That may be true, but when any living creature meets a violent end, it makes us sad," explained Stella. "At least it was a natural death. The predatory instinct of your cat is what saved us. We tried our best to catch the Deathmonger alive. We could do no more." Harry rolled his eyes at Lou. They were sharing the same thought. Only a hundred years on from 1979 and what a strange world they were a part of.

Juno gathered Dirtbag in her arms, petting him as Harry bent to pick up the dead wasp by one wing. Holding it at eye level, he stared the evil predator full in the face, while Lou held the pillowcase out tentatively at arm's length. After dropping the specimen inside, Harry took the pillowcase and swung it casually over his shoulder.

"At least we now have the proof Shizzle needs," he said, setting off back to the house.

An hour and a half later, Doctor Gideon Shizzle sat mortified in disbelief.

The monstrous dead insect lay before him on Stella's lawn, while Harry described seeing a first Deathmonger digging a tunnel in dry conditions, and then another wasp struggling in the wet.

Afterwards, Shizzle was led to the copse in time to see the rabbit hop dozily back to its burrow. Following Stella's injection with anti-venom it had made a full recovery, apart from a few missing tufts of fur. By the end of the tour, Dr Shizzle looked whiter than a sun-bleached pile of bones, and peered into the trees on high alert as he turned to Stella to offer his profound apologies.

"I was wrong to cross the Warnet species with the Tarantula Hawk wasp. I was wrong in carrying out the genetic modifications. My dream was to achieve a pesticide-free world, but my judgement was clouded. Look where that misplaced ambition has led."

Stella rested her hand gently on his shoulder. "At least no Deathmonger queens have been dispatched around the globe yet. The important thing now is to focus on ethically removing the entire species before any more break free from the compound to nest outside. If that were to happen, we really would be in trouble.

Shizzle hung his head in shame. "But, how can we destroy them? Without chemical sprays at our disposal those wasps will turn on us if we so much as enter the compound. Soon, there will be swarms of escaped Deathmongers flying at fifty kilometres per hour and capable of killing us all in the most grizzly manner."

"Don't worry, Dr Shizzle, Harry has an idea that just might work." Stella took Shizzle's arm and guided him over to the boy inventor, where the broken scientist stood staring and waiting for further enlightenment.

"We must breed fairy flies by the millions in labs throughout the world, Dr Shizzle," said Harry, bluntly. "Then we can plant separate batches to invade the Deathmonger nests and lay their eggs among the wasp larvae. In the meantime, water tankers must be introduced to the buffer zone, and robots programmed to douse the ground twice daily. That will stop the Deathmongers from digging tunnels while we bring our eradication plan to fruition.

Stella, who had stepped aside to make a Chipcom connection, suddenly joined in excitedly.

"I've just made contact with our laboratory network across the world and fast-tracked the multiplication of fairy flies. With the go-ahead to begin, we ought to have enough stock within a fortnight because of their short life cycle. That means phase one of Harry's plan is in the bag. Arranging the water tankers is also a simple enough task, it's phase three where the problems arise... The introduction of minute fairy flies into each and every Deathmonger nest. We must avoid harming any Warnets, they will be essential for protecting our precious food crops while the Deathmongers die out," she added solemnly.

After further discussion, the siblings decided to leave the scientists to complete the first two phases, agreeing to return in time for phase three. Harry offered the additional excuse that his parents were moving camp-sites; before he and Lou said their temporary goodbyes and stepped over the box hedge.

Both siblings were keen to see the Deathmonger adventure through, but were also looking forward to a brief spell of normality. After tucking Dirtbag inside his jacket, Harry mounted the trail bike behind his sister, and they rode back to the air raid shelters, then raced to the top of the grass bank. Waiting for the sun to set, the conversation inevitably turned to Grandpa Bert.

"I know we deserve to rest for a while, but I'm desperate to head back to 1879 in search of Grandpa," said Harry. "Bringing him home is really important to me." Lou smiled in agreement, but suddenly her head jerked and she stabbed a finger in the air.

"Lookout! A DDDD... Deathmonger!" Cowering away from the huge insect, buzzing nearby, she expected an equally panicked reaction from her brother, but instead, Harry glanced at the enormous wasp in an unconcerned manner.

"You're alright; that's only Alice. She's an everyday hornet queen. I met her while you were away. She's building a nest in the next air-raid shelter along. If we respect her, we'll get no bother, I'm sure."

Lou's shoulders relaxed for a second then tensed up again.

"You mean I've been living next to a giant hornet's nest, and you didn't think to mention it? What if I'd've wandered into the other bunker?"

"Well, you didn't, and if I'd've mentioned it, you'd've been like a cat on hot bricks, worrying about nothing. Alice is a part of the natural world. We should accept her as such." Lou sat flabbergasted as Harry pointed to the bright horizon and gestured towards Rivet.

"It's time for our jaunt along the Corridor of Light. I'll take Dirtbag in the car, you follow on the trail bike."

Entering the time portal, a part of Harry's mind was focused on the next level of their adventure. Finding Grandpa Bert after thirty-six years would be extremely hard. Multiple uncertainties flashed through his mind as he and Lou exited 2079 to arrive safely in 1979. Then, they cruised over to the farmhouse to be met by both parents.

Once indoors, they gathered around the dining room table and Lou quickly produced her photos of Bill and Stan with the strawberry jelly, which set them all screaming with laughter.

"Serves those two crooks right," said Mrs Scrambles, tucking into a hearty bowl of stew and dumplings, a little later. "Ooh, by the way, I've made your favourite, baked rice pudding with skin on, to celebrate the safe return of our entire family," she said.

Harry looked up with a slightly mischievous grin.

"You mean, the entire family, apart from Grandpa Bert?" he corrected. Mrs S looked moody at the remark and silence descended. Soon afterwards, the siblings retired gratefully to bed without mention of the Deathmonger situation.

CHAPTER 9.
THE RESCUE OF GRANDPA BERT

Two days later, Harry prepared to visit Grandma Gladys as promised. The prospect of a sleep-over left him underwhelmed. However, with Sophie and Rose due to visit Lou again, he was consoled by the thought that he would at least be avoiding a possible embarrassing encounter with his future wife.

Unfortunately, as Harry tossed his overnight bag onto Rivet's back seat, Rose arrived unexpectedly early. She immediately wandered over, carrying her suitcase, and Harry flushed bright red. He nodded briefly without speaking, then got into his car, but Rose's eyes followed with interest and she tapped on the side glass.

"Cool car," she began. Harry wound down the window by a single inch. "Nice colour, too. Did you fit the spotlights yourself?" Hoping against hope that his red face would soon fade, Harry made ready to answer but was saved by Lou, who approached quickly to crash the conversation.

"The tin can spotlights are definitely a Harry thing. Who else would think of something so daft? Or of cutting a massive hole in a perfectly good roof when it rains every day around here," she sniggered. "The plain fact is, Harry's inventions usually turn to disaster." Lou snorted with laughter, but Rose took no notice.

"The lights and colour scheme look pretty nifty if you ask me," she said shyly.

"Thank you," said Harry, smiling.

Lou scowled in frustration and Harry started the engine, then drove away. Ten minutes later, he pulled into Gladys' drive. Hearing the tyres on deep gravel, Harry's grandmother stood up in the garden between two rows of broad beans, placed both hands on her hips and arched her back in a stretch.

"Ahh, here he is. The scoundrel of the family," she said with a wrinkled grin. "And what mischief have you been up to lately?" Harry ambled over to lean on the handle of an upright spade, inserted at one end of a row of carrots.

"Nothing much to report at this precise minute, Grandma, but who knows? a mind-blowing event could occur at any time." Gladys laughed and flicked a finger in the direction of Rivet.

"There were no toys like that when I was

your age. All we had were skipping ropes and kiss chase games. Drop the handkerchief was my favourite. That's how I met your grandfather... He pretended not to be interested at first, but then I beat him at the Landlords Game; Monopoly as you know it. After that he suddenly turned keen. Proper handsome in those days was Bert." Gladys descended into a bout of quiet contemplation, and Harry took the opportunity to ask a less than tactful question.

"What would you do if Grandpa turned up now, after all these years?" Gladys replied to her grandson without a pause.

"Well... The fence needs painting, and I've a missing roof tile for a start. Now, shall we go and get a drink? I've made us a lovely blancmange, too," she cackled.

Harry followed into the house and entered the sitting room, breathing in a mixture of stagnant air and the scent of freshly cut flowers. After a minute, he crossed to the mantle piece and picked up a dog-eared photograph, sticking out from behind the clock. The picture featured his grandpa looking very dapper in a smart suit.

"Would you even recognise Grandpa Bert now, do you think? After thirty-six years, I mean?" asked Harry. Gladys continued cutting two slices of fruit cake as if she hadn't heard the question, then stared up at a stain on the ceiling for some time before speaking.

"Very good looking was Bert. Lovely blue eyes and a nicely shaped nose. He had a scar running from his left eye, halfway down one cheek. Got it as a boy, diving off a wall onto a concrete path. I'd recognise him, alright. He'd be getting a scar to match, on the other side of his face if he did turn up, believe you me." Harry cringed, then sat down heavily and changed the subject.

"Will you be making green tomato chutney this year, Grandma?" He loved Gladys' superb greenhouse. It was crammed with tomato plants, cucumbers, and melons; he liked the smell, too. Being a keen gardener himself, the conversation was kept on that subject for the rest of the visit.

After assisting Gladys with several garden duties, finally it was time to depart. As Harry walked towards the car, he turned slowly. "It's your birthday next week, Grandma. Maybe I'll treat you to a big surprise; what do you think?" Gladys glinted at her grandson fondly.

"You do that, dear," she said, chuckling, and with that, he reversed out of the drive, setting off along the farm lane.

Later that day, speaking to Lou, Harry raised their proposed search for Grandpa Bert. Lou wasted no time expressing her scepticism over the chances of finding him alive, but he was eager to paint a more optimistic picture.

"If Grandma Gladys is still alive, why not

Grandpa Bert? Anyway, the first thing to do in 1879 is search for a sign that he actually arrived. I'd have left a message just in case someone came looking. Finding some sort of proof would be a great start."

"What? Like a note saying, 'Grandpa woz 'ere," taunted Lou. "PS. I went that way. Let's face it, Harry, Grandpa could be anywhere by now. Or dead. And we'd have to hide the trail bike... There'd be no riding around searching for him. We'd be on foot and it'd take ages."

"Fair point," said Harry. "Perhaps we should disguise the motorbike... As a horse, maybe? If we drove fast enough, no one would spot the engine."

"Oh really? A horse with two wheels, revving past people at seventy miles per hour. Never a batted eyelid, I'm sure... You tonker." Despite Lou's initially negative comments, after further discussion she relented and agreed to camouflaging the motorbike, after all. Harry had soon fashioned a paper mâché horse's head around the headlamp and draped a cardboard saddle over the petrol tank to cover the engine. Then, with a bailer twine tail covering the number plate, the disguise was complete. They were all set for time travel back into the nineteenth century.

Later, at teatime, each of them tucked away large portions of toad in the hole covered in rich gravy as Harry broached Grandpa Bert's rescue with his father.

"It sounds like a good idea, camouflaging the motorbike, at least for when you first arrive. We can't go upsetting history, however important the mission. You've got my blessing to search for Grandpa on one condition. You pay heed to your mother's words of warning." With that, Mrs S took over sternly.

"There'll be no taking of unnecessary risks and you must promise to come straight home at the first sign of trouble."

"Don't worry, Mum. We'll be super careful, just like we were in 2079; you can count on it," said Lou. Anyway, what could go wrong? Travelling backwards in time is way less risky. We already know the world didn't come to an end. In fact, I expect life was pretty dull during the nineteenth century in rural Lincolnshire."

Their mother gave a reluctant nod as her children headed upstairs early, setting their alarms for 4 am.

The following morning, Harry leapt out of bed and ran to the window, but his face dropped at the sight of raindrops splashing hard against the glass. After getting dressed he met Lou downstairs.

"We still have two hours until sunrise, the rain might blow over," said Lou, stepping outside behind Harry, who had stopped suddenly in his tracks.

"Sunrise," He uttered, cradling his head with

both hands in a most peculiar manner.

"Sunrise, what?" snapped Lou as Harry turned to face her with a despairing look on his face.

"Grandpa went through the portal at sunset. What are we doing here at 4 AM?" When the blunder sank in, Lou collapsed onto the wet grass, allowing raindrops to run down her cheeks until eventually, she grinned up at her brother.

"What a pair of idiots."

"Well, at least the rain has more time to stop," replied Harry as the bedraggled pair gathered themselves, and headed back to bed.

Later that day, rasping towards the shelters on a noisy horse, it was still raining. Puddle water soaked their trousers but arriving at the Orthostats, things looked more promising. A thin orange strip soon appeared beyond a bank of clouds on the western horizon and the sun burst through, instantly forming the magical Corridor of Light between the stone rows. Peering into the gleaming time-tunnel, the sheer enormity of their mission hit Harry, and both eyes welled up. His mind switched to Juno. He had met her through the portal, and she now felt a fundamental part of his family. Harry hoped that the same would be true of Bert and that, unlike Juno, Grandpa could safely accompany him home.

Lou, though, had a very different train of thought, details of which she piped up dreamily to

Harry.

"Think of the extra Christmas presents coming our way if we do bring Grandpa back with us," she said, rubbing her hands together gleefully and mounting the motorbike. Harry sniffed, drew the back of his hand across his eyes, and smiled at his sister.

"Trust you to think of that," he said, throwing one leg over the soggy cardboard saddle and gripping his sister's shoulders tightly. Lou kick-started the engine and they entered the Corridor of Light at sixty-five miles per hour, a magnetic flash signalling their arrival in 1879. After applying the brakes hard, she steered immediately through thick undergrowth.

Along the way, the sodden cardboard horse collapsed into several mushy heaps on the floor, but ignoring the mess, Harry opened his rucksack and pulled out a two-man tent. "Let's pitch in the middle of this thicket before it gets dark. We'll be well hidden in case there are people around at first light." An hour later, cosily tucked inside sleeping bags, they listened to the sound of silence and quickly fell asleep.

Harry was first to wake the next morning and he lay still, wondering how to go about tracking their grandpa. As Lou began to stir, he shook her fully awake.

"Here, take some food. We need to get going."

He passed over a Texan bar and a bag of chicken crisps. "Enjoy," he said, forcing a handful of salt and vinegar crisps into his own mouth, then biting into a Curly Wurly and mashing both items together with his teeth.

A few minutes later, Harry unzipped the tent cautiously and crawled through the undergrowth until the Orthostats came into view. The bleating of sheep filled the air, and the familiar smell of bluebells made him sneeze as he stood up, with Lou emerging behind him.

"Keep the noise down," she whispered, yawning and stretching both arms into the air. "You do realise, this is going to be like looking for a needle in a haystack. Grandpa could be dead, in hospital or both. We should check some graves in the churchyard first; that could save us a lot of bother. And one more thing. How are we supposed to recognise Bert if we do see him?"

"First things first." replied Harry. "Let's find some proof that he actually arrived. There maybe a message written with pebbles on the floor or something?"

As Harry began to search, Lou wandered after him giving a negative commentary.

"Any loose stones would have been kicked all over the place by animals after thirty-six years. We'd better hope Grandpa thought of something better than that for an idea.

"Okay, how about a message written on an immovable object, then... Like an Orthostat? The limestone ones would be easiest to mark."

They headed over to the stone cluster, trampled down the brambles and stood back to let the early morning light illuminate the pale face of one of the centrally positioned limestones.

"There," yelled Harry, stepping forward to run his fingertips over faint etchings, barely visible on the rock.

A rectangular box with the number, one, scratched above it, contained several lines of writing which Harry read out:

Bert Scrambles 1943

Trapped in 1843

Find box 2...

"Box two, find box two," Harry yelled at Lou, who hopped across the Corridor to the opposite limestone, before reading the follow-up message, excitedly.

1846

working at stables

follow tree markers

"Wow," said Lou, "Let's look for a tree with an arrow or something carved on it. Grandpa's left us a kind of long-lasting paper chase." She jogged over to a stout oak, nearby, with Harry setting off in the opposite direction, but after scouring dozens of tree trunks, neither one could find any arrows. Finally, the dejected siblings regrouped at the camp-site.

"Maybe the first tree has been cut down?" suggested Harry. "We need to extend our search. Once we find a single arrow, it will point us towards the next tree, and so-on."

"But there are hundreds of trees within a mile radius of the Orthostats. Finding a first mark could take hours on foot. And even then, Grandpa's stables could be thirty miles away, which would mean days of walking," said Lou dejectedly.

"I say we borrow a horse," said Harry. "There must be plenty of them about, cars haven't been invented yet, remember. We'd find Grandpa in no time on a horse."

Harry felt a strange tingle running along his spine as he uttered the words, 'find Grandpa.' Having now found definitive evidence that Grandpa was not killed in the second world war, he felt positive, and Lou also perked up at the idea of riding a horse, nodding her head enthusiastically.

"Good idea, getting a horse. I could give you a backy. After all, I'm the expert. With hedges and fences to jump, we don't want any broken bones. Chewing on a stick while they sawed off your leg would be no fun, and Mum'd be none too happy if you arrived home like Tiny Tim; on crutches." Harry grinned a half-grin. It was true, his sister was a much more accomplished rider than him.

They set off down the lane, past dozens of small fields, each with neatly laid hedges, chuckling pheasants and squawking crows until, arriving at Minute's hill, Harry made a suggestion. "Let's head over to the limekiln. I bet it's a working pit, here in 1879. They're bound to have horses." Lou shrugged, and soon both were walking through the substantial wrought iron gates marking the edge of Fryston park. Ducking by the farm worker's cottages, they skirted the carp pond and entered the woods. Suddenly, Lou flagged Harry down and pulled him behind a tree. The sound of voices echoed through the woodland, along with an intermittent squeaking as three open railway trucks moved slowly along a set of tracks, all pulled by a single shire horse. The wagons were piled high with white powder.

"Hydrated lime, the predecessor to cement," whispered Harry. It's made by burning limestone at high temperature inside the pit."

Just then, a voice rang out through the trees.

"Oiy, you boys. Behind that tree. Come on out, now."

Harry and Lou stepped nervously into the open to face an elderly man leading the shire horse with a rope. After applying a brake on the wagons and tethering the animal, the man wandered over while the heavy horse snuffled among the nettles.

"Ain't no one warned you 'bout playin round 'ere? Tis dangerous. One slip and that'd be the end of thee. Burned to a cinder in the pit wiyout a trace."

"Oh," said Harry. "Thanks for the warning but we weren't playing; we were looking for our grandfather, Bert Scrambles. Do you know him?" The man hesitated and took on a thoughtful expression.

"That name do ring a bell. A long time since, mind. Nigh on forty years I reckon. Aay, he worked here a while, that'd be right. Bert Scamberls, you mean. A man full o' tall stories as I recall. Said he were lost. Said he were looking for a way home. Talked of magic and other daft stuff. Went to work in a stable yard in the end."

"Do you know where?" snatched Lou, "We have to find him; it's urgent."

The man looked agitated.

"I telled ye once. It were forty year since. Now, off wee ye. I've work to do."

"Well, can you lend us a horse then?... Please?" begged Harry, bluntly. "Just for one afternoon. We'll bring it straight back, I promise." The man laughed and taking off his cap, scratched his head.

"Yee've a rum cheek, I'll gi yee that. There be my own horse I suppose, but she be tall. Seventeen hands. Neither one of ye could mount, much less ride her," he stated.

"I've ridden plenty of big horses in gymkhanas,"

spurted Lou indignantly."

The man's brow furrowed.

"Jim who?" He let out a deep sigh and continued, "Listen... For all yer brass necked cheek, I'll do ye a deal. Come see my horse, top of the hill, and if ye can mount her and jump the hedge by the pond wiyout a fall, I'll lend her ye. Can't say fairer than that..."

The siblings nodded enthusiastically as they followed the old man up the hill. "My name's Wilfred. Wilf, for short, 'ow bout you?" Harry and Lou introduced themselves and arriving at the top of the hill, watched as Wilf pulled a lever at the front of each wagon, tipping the lime by the side of the track. Several men with shovels immediately began filling hessian sacks, while others tied and loaded the full bags onto a cart. Meanwhile, a small boy of about Harry's age added a large scoop of oats to a nosebag, then clambered onto the second rung of a nearby fence and pulled two of the bag straps over the horse's head.

Wilfred stepped away from the train, beckoning Harry and Lou. "There be my horse. She be a real beauty by the name of Carla." He directed his voice at Lou. "Go on then, let's see what yer made of, boy." Wilfred flicked his wrist, and Lou combed back her hair with the fingers of both hands as she walked over. Noticing that the stirrups were well out of reach, she turned to Harry.

"Give us a bunk up, would you?" Harry backed himself into the horse's belly and clasped both hands below the stirrup so that Lou could step on his joined-up palms. Grabbing the saddle, she sprang onto the horse's back. The man looked impressed as Lou stroked the horse's neck reassuringly, and he muttered in a low voice while handing over the reins.

"So far, be so good, but now we'll see." Without warning, he slapped the horse's rump and it set off at a gallop across the field. Lou climbed high in the stirrups as the powerful horse set her heart racing. Gradually she gained control of the frightening animal, circled around and headed for the hedge in front of the carp pond. Under Lou's direction, Carla jumped the barrier beautifully but there was a shock in store. Over the hedge, they were confronted by the steep bank of the carp pond just a few yards further on. Lou pulled Carla sharply around, avoiding the murky water and cantered back through an open gate to the watching workmen, who began a round of applause as they crowded in closer.

"Well done, lad," said Wilfred. "Thought you was in fer a proper dousing there, but, a deal's a deal, so take my horse and be sure to have her back by the end of the day."

Lou smiled. "Thank you, Sir, we appreciate your help."

"I likes to see a boy wiya bit o' spunk," replied

Wilf as Lou trotted Carla over towards Harry who was perched on the top rung of the nearby fence. After pulling her brother roughly onto the horse, they wheeled to face Wilfred who offered two, paper-wrapped objects, taken from a bag hung on a gatepost. "Spect ye'll both be hungry. Here, take these cheese cobs."

"Thanks. We'll get your horse back as soon as we can," said Lou, trotting away up the lane to circle the nearest tree, while happily munching her handmade bread roll.

By the day's end, having circumnavigated every tree within half a mile of the Orthostats, they had found nothing. Forced to head back to the lime pit, Wilf registered the forlorn expressions on both faces.

"No joy, then?" he asked. "I saw ye circling they trees, earlier. Why were that?" Harry explained, and the man's face lit up. "I seen one of they carved arrows on a tree, years back... Top-end of the green lane, past they big standing stones; the ones Bert reckoned be magic."

Noticing the siblings had suddenly cheered up, Wilfred pointed to the cottages at the top of Minute's hill. "Let us know if ye find yer grandpa. Mine's the end cottage. Drop-in. My Lauretta's good for a plate of grub any time." After saying their goodbyes, Harry and Lou jogged off up the lane, chattering in full voice.

"Things are looking up," began Harry. "And I have to admit, you're not bad on a horse, either. Bit lairy over the big hedges, mind."

With the sun low in the sky, they decided to light a camp-fire and settle in for the night. Both agreed that tomorrow would be a make-or-break day.

Following a breakfast of buttered crackers, consumed whilst hurrying up the lane in search of the first arrow, they separated to check every tree in the area. Still, neither sibling found a direction indicator of any kind.

"That's typical," began Lou. "We get our hopes up and they're dashed again. Might as well head home if you ask me. Let's face it, We've no chance of ever finding Grandpa." Harry sighed and dropped, cross-legged, onto the grass at the foot of an oak tree. After stroking his chin for several minutes, his face suddenly lit up.

"Of course! We've been looking in the wrong place," he exclaimed.

"Wrong place? What wrong place? A tree's a tree and there are no arrows, durgh. How do you mean, wrong place?"

"I mean, some trees are older than others," said Harry, "And I dare bet that Bert carved his arrows onto the trunks of young trees. They'd be less likely to get cut down or succumb to disease. It's plain common sense, really."

"Yes, but we've checked every tree for miles,

young and old," snapped Lou.

"But not higher up," cried Harry. Grandpa's young trees have had thirty-six years to grow taller. The arrows will be much further up the trunk by now." Jumping to his feet, he craned his neck into the branches above their heads.

"Look there. I've been sat under an arrow all along," he exclaimed. Lou followed Harry's eyes and sure enough, a small, hand-carved mark could be seen pointing into the distance. After staring, gob-smacked, at the feature for several seconds, she sprinted off, shouting back to her brother.

"Come on then, let's find the next one."

Harry and Lou moved quickly from tree to tree, easily following the high pointers until reaching a busy road with several horses and carts travelling in either direction.

"Ermine street, the old Roman road," said Harry. "Look how straight it is. According to that last arrow, we should cross over and head towards those farm buildings over there." He pointed ahead to rooftops, visible above the hedge line.

"Wow, I wonder if that's where Grandpa works," speculated Lou, the pitch of her voice rising to match her excitement. "I can definitely see horses in the fields over there." A lump formed in Harry's throat at the thought as they crossed the road and followed a narrow bridleway between two hedges in the direction of the buildings.

The bushes were eventually replaced by wooden fences, beyond which, horses with jockeys high in the stirrups rode around the fields. Soon the bridleway opened into a farmyard. Harry marched confidently towards a smart building with a clock tower situated between two smaller stable blocks.

"You looking for work?" came a sudden voice from one of the barns. "Cuz the office is over there." A man's outstretched arm appeared over a stable door, pointing across the yard. The siblings changed course obediently and passed a set of glass doors beneath the clock tower. Their eyes were instantly drawn inside to a smart wooden dresser with several silver cups arranged on its shelves. Continuing across the yard, they knocked on the office door.

"Enter," came a stern voice. Harry opened the door to find a middle-aged man seated behind a dark oak desk. He beckoned impatiently. "Come in. Are you the new stable hands?" He watched both siblings go red in the face with embarrassment, and Lou answered coyly.

"No sir, sorry sir. We're searching for a man who works here."

"Well, come on, chop chop, I haven't got all day. We've a race to win. Who do you mean."

"Well," said Harry, "His name is probably Bert Scrambles."

"Probably? Well, is it or isn't it?..... If you mean

Bert Scamberls? He's our head trainer and a very busy man... That's him in the paddock, putting the top horses through their paces." The man gestured through a window to a field, visible between two barns. "We've a big big race at the weekend and right now, there's no time to lose. You'd be better off coming back in a week or two. Now, go on, shoo." The man ushered them out of his office and Harry marched acceptingly towards the bridleway, in the opposite direction to the racing paddock.

"We can't go without seeing Grandpa, now," chuntered Lou. "Not after coming all this way."

The track soon curved out of sight of the office at which point Harry ducked behind the barn and Lou followed. Skirting quickly back around to the paddock area, gruff voices could be heard behind a tidy laurel hedge.

"Yes, Longshadow is our strongest colt, but Brightlight, the young filly, has more potential if only she can be trained hard before the race. What we need is a rider capable of putting her through her paces over the next few days. By then, Charlie's leg should be strong enough and he can take over. Without Brightlight being properly prepared, Longshadow is our best bet for Saturday." The voice tailed off and an all too familiar one answered back.

"Okay, Brian. Remember what I said. Keep trying different jockeys out. There must be someone to suit Brightlight. Now, let's get on."

Lou glanced at Harry, who had gone very white in the face. "What's up? You look like you've seen a ghost," she whispered.

"That was Dad's voice. Didn't you recognise it?"

Lou's jaw dropped as she considered Harry's words. He was right, the voice was similar to their own father, but she hadn't noticed at the time. Instead, an intense daydream had invaded her mind. A dream in which she was riding a real racehorse to victory.

With the sudden crunch of footsteps on nearby gravel, both children ducked further into the leafy hedge as one of the men marched away. The second man followed but then stopped right in front of the siblings. Raising the palm of his hand, he pushed it against his forehead, closed his eyes and stood stock-still. A long scar could be seen running from one eye all the way down his left cheek.

"Grandpa Bert, Bert Scrambles?" said Harry in an involuntary outburst. The startled man peered into the hedge, and the siblings backed out from the undergrowth then walked around to meet their grandfather.

"You followed the arrows, then?" he asked calmly.

"Yes, after we saw your messages on the Orthostats."

"Orthostats." repeated the man. "That word was in a book I once read. A very, very long time ago."

"I know," said Harry. "And, when you stood those Orthostats back up, the time portal was reactivated, which is how you got here from 1943. We've come to rescue you... To take you home to Grandma Gladys."

"Home? Home to my Gladys? Yes, of course, but how is she?" Grandpa Bert suddenly looked weak. "I need to sit down. come with me." He staggered slowly towards the clock tower with Harry and Lou following until the man from the office suddenly yelled in their direction.

"Oiy, I told you kids not to disturb Bert."

"It's okay, Fred; it's alright. They're friends of mine. Don't worry." Fred nodded and closed his office door quietly.

Stepping inside the clock tower building, they passed the numerous silver cups and beautifully framed portraits of horses hung on every wall. Bert waved them into a large room with a bed at one end. Easy chairs were grouped around a stone fireplace nearer the door, and he shouted down the hallway. "Tea for three, sandwiches and cakes, please, Joey." Closing the door, he sat down next to his grandchildren.

"Well, well. Gladys is alive, and she's your grandmother. Now that I can't fall down, you'd better tell me how she is?"

"Grandma's fine," said Harry. "I spent time with her just the other day. She told me about the scar on your cheek from when you leapt off the wall as a boy." Bert's eyes glazed over as he listened, then cleared his throat.

"Yes, It was a tantrum, an act of defiance, aged six. Mum wouldn't buy me an ice cream and I made the threat. She refused to change her mind so I went ahead and did it. But never mind that. I need to know why I couldn't get home through this time portal thingy? I tried to walk the other way so many times but it was no good. Thirty-six years I've been stuck here."

Harry stood up, and pacing back and forth, passed on what he knew. "Directly after you walked along the Corridor of Light, your son, our father, John Scrambles, removed an Orthostat from the 1943 end. He had no idea that this would deactivate the time portal for walking. Neither did he know you had already walked along the Corridor of Light at sunset. When a German bomb went off nearby, just a few minutes after your disappearance, the Ministry of Defence labelled you missing/presumed dead."

"Ah, I see. That makes sense, but if the portal was deactivated, how did you get here?"

"We found out that travelling faster through the portal compensates for the missing stone. We came here at sixty-five miles per hour on my trail bike. Don't worry, it's well hidden and ready for our safe return home," replied Lou. Grandpa took a sip of his tea and picked up a sandwich.

"A motorbike, eh. Help yourselves to cake and tell me your names. What should I be calling my grandchildren?"

The siblings introduced themselves and moved on with stories of their other adventures involving Bill and Stan. Finally, after a lot of raucous laughter, Grandpa Bert crossed to the mantle-piece, opened a wooden box and removed a sheet of paper.

"The day I arrived here from 1943, I set down my experience on paper, writing as if it happened to someone else, to avoid awkward questions should anyone read it." He handed the piece of paper to Harry, "Here, you might like to take a look, later on, but for now we've more important things to discuss.

Lou, eagerly addressed her grandfather. "Yes. tell me about this big race then, Grandpa? We overheard you talking about two horses... Longshadow and Brightlight. Did you train both yourself? What a fantastic way to make your mark on a new world."

"We've been fortunate in producing a few winners over the years, but Saturday will be our biggest race yet. Two thoroughbreds are each in with a chance of winning the Trantham cup and a three thousand guinea purse. Longshadow will be ridden by my adopted son, Joey Tindle, and we also have a feisty filly named Brightlight. She has struggled to find a mount. No prizes for guessing how I came up with the horse's names... Unfortunately, our champion Jockey, Charlie Clarke, is recovering from a leg injury and Brightlight shows no response to any other jockey. She's the type of horse that needs to be bossed."

Lou's eyes lit up. "I'll give her a run out if you like, Gramps. I love fast horses," she said cheekily. Grandpa Bert grinned.

"Thanks, but Brightlight is a very skittish horse, Louise. With respect, I doubt you'd even manage to mount her." Lou looked a little deflated, and Harry winked in her direction, then addressed his grandfather.

"How about a small wager," he said. "If Lou mounts your horse without using steps or climbing a fence, she gets a chance. I can certainly vouch for her being a capable rider and even better at bossing."

Grandpa Bert shrugged.

"Well, alright then, we'll see, but no steps and no climbing up the fence, that's the deal." He spat on his hand and offered it to Lou, who shook it firmly. After filing over to the paddock, Bert leaned over the rail and beckoned a small man on a tall, slender racehorse. The horse trotted over, and the man dismounted, handing the reins to Bert. "I'd like my new lad here, to try out on Brightlight while you get your lunch," said Grandpa. "Thanks, Tim. Be back in forty minutes, please." The jockey passed his whip to Lou and smiled.

"Go careful; she's a wild one," he said. "You'll need to show her who's in charge, right away." Lou nodded without speaking. She was well aware that in 1879, a female rider would be expected to ride side-saddle and had no intention of doing that.

Approaching the horse with a wry smile, Lou's mind was filled with positive thoughts. Getting aboard this horse would be a doddle compared to Carla, even without a bunk up. Brightlight was under sixteen hands tall.

Once in the saddle, Lou patted the horse's neck, stroking its mane gently. The horse neighed and stamped a foot impatiently as Lou whispered firmly into one ear, then Grandpa Bert spoke.

"Take things easy for the first lap, Lou, she's a valuable horse and you're an even more valuable grandchild." He handed over the reins, then offered the whip.

"I won't be needing that," said Lou, wheeling the horse around and setting off across the open paddock. Brightlight soon accelerated to a gallop and Lou leaned forward whispering constant encouragement in the filly's ear. "Let's show them what we can do," she hissed as Brighlight charged past Harry and Grandpa Bert, who was performing a drum roll on the fence rails in excitement. After three more laps, Lou slowed to a canter and trotted over, calling down from the horse. "She's great. And non too sluggish, either."

Grandpa's face glowed in response.

"It seems Brightlight likes your approach. Only Charlie has ever brought her on like that, before. I'd like you to stay on here at the stables for a few days to work her some more? You could really help her chances. Of course, both you and Harry are invited to watch the big race on Saturday. I promise to travel home through the portal straight afterwards."

Lou turned away and pumped a fist, then spun back around, agreeing to Grandpa's suggestion. With Harry also nodding in excitement, Bert called over to a man wheeling a barrow full of hay across the yard. "Hey, Sammy, please ask Franky to prepare two rooms, one each for my guests, Harry and Lou." The man parked the barrow, scuttling away and shortly afterwards, the siblings found themselves relaxing on comfortable beds in the cosy accommodation block.

Every morning for the next three days, Lou gave Brightlight her morning workout while Harry and Bert watched from the sidelines. By the end of the week, there was a noticeable improvement in pace from the horse.

"I can't believe the transformation," said Bert to

Harry. "It's as if horse and rider have known each other for years, Brightlight is responding so well. Only Charlie has ever formed such a bond with that horse."

Between sessions, Harry and Lou continued to tell Grandpa Bert about their life, including how their parents had first met. Bert reciprocated with tales of his own, which were centred on a lifetime's dedication to horses. Then, on the eve of the big race, champion jockey, Charlie Clarke arrived at the weigh-in. At three pounds overweight, a look of concern crossed Bert's face and he explained to the siblings that the Trantham purse was to be run over a gruelling two miles, with the weather set to be hot.

"The extra weight will put enormous pressure on the horse and on Charlie's leg, which we've been resting. His general fitness could also be an issue in the heat," said Bert as the jockey mounted the horse for a trial run. "Any pain today, and Brightlight will have to be withdrawn from the race," he warned.

Charlie set off at a canter, rising cautiously from the saddle to put full weight on the stirrups. Then, after breaking into a slow gallop, horse and rider gradually increased speed for three laps before returning to face Bert. Lou stood behind her grandfather with her fingers crossed, secretly praying for bad news, but Charlie's cheerful report dashed her hopes all too soon.

"My leg feels great and the horse is on top form. All credit to this new young rider of yours. He's done a cracking job." Charlie turned to Lou, who managed a half-smile, despite seething inside.

"That's great news, Charlie" said Bert before turning to his grandchildren, "I've organised prime seats for tomorrow in the grandstand to watch the entire days racing. It will be a glamorous occasion. Lord Scantlebury, the owner of the stables is coming. Top tea and cakes will be available all day long."

"Wow, that sounds fantastic, Grandpa," said Harry, but Lou's attempt at sounding equally enthusiastic, quickly degenerated into an irritable scowl.

At the crack of dawn the following day, the stable yard was an explosion of activity. Every racehorse had to be exercised before transportation to Harrowby fields racetrack, and Lou was forced to drag herself out of bed early to work Brightlight. Afterwards, she barely glanced at the huddle of men who surrounded Bert until Harry beckoned her and Brightlight over.

Approaching at a slow, moping pace, Lou noticed that Grandpa Bert looked serious.

"I'm afraid it's bad news, Lou. Charlie can barely move his leg this morning; it stiffened up overnight. There's not much point in exercising Brightlight anymore because she won't be running." Bert hesitated and looked Lou straight in the eye.

"Unless you fancy a try, that is?"

For some moments, Lou kept a straight face, while inside her head was a mess. This offer was beyond her wildest dreams but fear of failure also registered highly. Riding Brightlight in an actual race was a huge ask for a fifteen year old girl. As she mulled over the dreamy proposition, her grandfather's voice was a distant echo.

"We'd enter you under a different name, of course... Lou Scamberls would be fitting, and I'm game if you are," he said quietly.

Lou pulled herself together and replied with confidence.

"Joey and Longshadow make a great team. They will surely take over as bookies favourite, so the pressure will be off me. I'd love to ride Brightlight, Grandpa."

"Perfect," said Bert. "Joey is my adopted son. He started out as a stable hand fifteen years ago, gradually learning the ropes. Nowadays, he trains as well as he rides. After today's race, I plan to retire and pass my job at the stables to Joey. I can think of no better way to end my career than watching you two race head to head. It'll be a day to remember and I'll be equally proud of both of you, whatever the outcome."

Lou turned and cantered away, shouting over her

shoulder as she broke into a gallop.

"Thanks for the pep talk, Gramps. Tell Joey, I may be the underdog, but I still intend to win."

Several hours later, Lou was fully kitted out in colourful racing attire and sat astride Brightlight, next to Longshadow and eight other runners.

The tape dropped with Joey on Longshadow shooting ahead as expected. Lou found herself pressed hard against the rails on the inside of the track. She was behind the horse in fourth position with three others boxing her in. It was now or never for the opportunity to take control of the race, and Lou whispered into the ear of Brightlight, then prepared to take that chance.

"We must go back to go forward," she hissed, relaxing the reins and dropping off the pace. Falling to eighth position, she cleared the group, then swung out wide with Brightlight responding to a gentle tap of the neck. As they surged along the straight, Lou panted, "GO GO GO," and lifted herself high in the stirrups, charging past five horses in quick succession.

Placed third ahead of the next bend, they tucked in behind the horse in front, passing the grandstand to the roar of the huge crowd. Lou's spirits rose as she mulled her strategy with one lap to go. They would stay neatly in third until the final bend, then let rip.

Lou pictured herself twisting the throttle of her

trail bike. She sensed the adrenalin rush, the sheer exhilaration, the burst of petrol-powered speed. Praying that Brightlight had had a good breakfast, she knew that all of the horse's energy reserves would be required for those last seconds of racing.

Towards the centre of the course, hundreds of working-class spectators filled the infield. They clutched small scraps of paper and cheered her on. These ordinary folk had put their money on the unheard of, replacement jockey. An outsider, a long shot, and Lou prayed for them all. A win against the odds would mean such a lot for them. She had to deliver.

Switching concentration back to the race, her heart pounded and her lungs felt fit to burst. Both legs felt like jelly as long beads of sweat poured down her back, while the front of her tunic remained dry as desert sand, rippling and flapping in the wind.

As horse and mount rounded the final bend, Lou's mind was a blur. She stroked Brightlight's neck, the calming measure being as much for her as the horse. Then she waited. She waited until, with a sudden flick of the reins the team of two swerved from behind the horse in front and galloped level.

Lou rose and fell in the saddle, leaning ever further forward. "Focus on first," she whispered. "Focus on first. We have one more horse to beat."

Brightlight stretched her neck, surging into second position, directly behind Longshadow, while Lou pressed her head tightly into the horse's flowing mane. The erupting crowd roared and the people scuttled forwards in the stands. They stretched their torso's over the rails, shook sweaty fists and waved betting slips as the two front runners flew by, yards ahead of the rest of the field.

Finally, the entire grandstand rose to its feet as Brightlight lengthened her stride, reaching the back of Longshadow. The two-furlong marker flashed by and Lou realised that just four hundred metres remained. Now was the time for a final push.

Tapping the neck of her horse three times as she'd done every day in practice, Lou gave the signal and the horse's ears pricked up. Charging forwards, Lou was dizzy with adrenalin. "Go, go, go," she first whispered, then screamed as Brightlight moved effortlessly ahead of Longshadow and accelerated towards the line.

Joey glanced frantically sideways to witness Lou moving past and his face melted into a smile of recognition. He'd been beaten fair and square.

After crossing the line, the horses slowed and both jockeys dropped into their saddles, cantering over to the owner's enclosure. Lou's eyes were misty, but she could see Harry, jumping up and down in slow motion, while Grandpa Bert stood stock-still, the tears rolling down his cheeks.

A group of over over-excited reporters armed with box cameras clamoured to get pictures of the winner and someone took hold of Brightlight's reins, allowing Lou to dismount. Removing the saddle, a cloud of steam rose as Brightlight was led away to the horses enclosure, and turning to Harry and Bert, Lou raised her arms. She sprung into the air, then locked into a happy embrace, soon joined by Joey, who was full of congratulations.

"Well done. I knew we had a pair of good uns, but first and second? What a race. Who'd have thought it?" He patted Lou on the shoulder. "We must complete the formalities, now." With that, they bounded off to be weighed, while Bert was beckoned over to the winning horse, where twenty minutes of press fervour ensued.

Afterwards, Lord Scantlebury, the ecstatic owner of Brightlight, invited everyone to the Grandstand for more celebrations, all of which continued long into the evening, rounding off the memorable day.

The following morning, with the rejoicing done, they were all back at the stable yard. Bert took Joey to one side and invited him to take over as head trainer. He took the idea well, happy to step into his father's shoe's and understanding Bert's wish to spend more time with his new family.

Later, in planning their exodus from the nineteenth century, it was decided that Harry would take Grandpa home, first. He would return the following evening for Lou, who was happy to spend an extra day at the stables alongside Joey, with whom she had become firm friends.

Once Bert had said his goodbyes to the yard staff, he and Harry set off towards the Orthostats. Along the way, Harry spoke of the kind man at the Lime pit and described the bamboozling effect of the marker arrows moving up the tree trunks over the years.

"Ah, you mean Wilfred Topper," said Grandpa. "He and his good wife, Lauretta, took me in when I first arrived. Wilf gave me a job bagging lime at the pit. It was hard work, but they are indeed generous folk."

Upon reaching the stones, Harry wheeled the motorbike into the open and sitting confidently astride it, flicked out the kick-start then turned on the ignition. When a hefty boot yielded no more than a loud cough and a backfire, Harry made three more attempts, looking gradually more concerned. After double-checking the petrol was turned on, he kicked the starter once more, then turned hesitantly to Grandpa Bert.

"I think the spark plug needs cleaning. It's nothing to worry about, I've a plug spanner under the seat." But in reality, Harry was worried, he was very worried. Hastily removing a small tool kit and unscrewing the spark plug, he held it up to the light. His startled look immediately told Grandpa Bert that something was seriously wrong.

Harry gulped and spurted out the problem. "The electrode has burned away. The engine must have overheated when the mock cardboard saddle covered the cylinder head as we travelled along the Corridor of Light. "I tried to disguise the bike as a horse," he admitted in despair.

"Urmm. Not a smart idea, covering an air-cooled engine," said Bert. "The chances of us finding a replacement spark plug are pretty slim, too," he added. Motorbikes haven't been invented yet!"

Harry grinned limply at his grandpa, but the plain fact was obvious. All three family members were trapped in 1879.

CHAPTER 10. CAN HARRY DO IT?

"What do you mean, we're stuck here on account of your daft horse disguise, the one I warned you against?" snapped Lou in a thunderous voice..."

Grandpa Bert jumped to Harry's defence, trying to sound optimistic. "Don't worry, Louise. We've two things in our favour this time, unlike when I got trapped before." Lou remained stony-faced.

"With all due respect, Grandpa, by my reckoning, we've had it. Reaching the 65mph, needed to activate the portal is impossible without a motorbike." Grandpa Bert shrugged, remaining entirely calm as he replied.

"Yes, but we now know it is possible to compensate for failings in the portal with ideas like travelling faster than walking pace to generate extra energy. I'm sure with Harry's inventive expertise, we'll soon work something out."

"Inventive expertise? Are you kidding? Harry's top ideas don't cut the mustard when faced with the simplest of problems to solve. I wouldn't get your hopes up Grandpa. Huh."

"I have full confidence in Harry," replied Grandpa, "Just as I did in you, riding Brightlight the other day."

Bigged up by his Grandpa's vote of confidence, Harry could feel a crazy scheme brewing and without hesitation, he splurged out the details. "Listen, you two. When Stan and Bill got the portal working with five stones present, they adjusted the travel speed upwards. We need to apply the same logic in reverse to find a solution, here."

"What do you mean? You're talking nonsense again, Harry."

"I mean, increase the total number of Orthostats, thus reducing the necessary speed of travel, back down."

"Eh?" screamed Lou. "How are we sposed to reinstate a five-ton Orthostat that's buried under Dad's workshop in a different time dimension. So, you think you're Ali Bongo the magician, now, do you?" She sat down heavily, shaking her head in disbelief.

"No, we don't need to reinstate the Orthostat at the 1979 end of the portal," said Harry. "We add an extra one this end instead... It seems to me that portal power is generated by the combined forces of light and magnetic energy at BOTH ends of the Corridor, not just one end."

"Well, even if that's true, where will this spare Orthostat come from, then? And how can we move it to the Corridor without heavy machinery?"

"There's no need," said Harry. "We can build our replica on the spot, bit by bit. In fact, I was thinking of knocking up two while we're at it? My design of Orthostat won't be as powerful as an original, so a pair would be better. It would give us a fighting chance of reducing the speed requirement to, say, 25mph, which should be enough to get us out of trouble." Lou jumped to her feet and stalked to the far end of the room, pivoting aggressively on both feet as she attacked Harry's notion.

"25mph? Oh! So, you can run at 25mph then, can you? AND piggy-back Grandpa at the same time? Because he most certainly can't go that fast on his own... No offence, Grandpa."

"Not me personally, no," said Harry. "But a horse would ace it. They reach forty miles per hour when racing. Twenty-five will be a doddle, even two-up."

"That's true enough," muttered Grandpa from the chair next to Harry. "And, it's certainly worth a try," he glanced at Lou, whose expression signalled another frank exchange of views between her and Harry was about to kick off.

"Okay, so what will we be using to build

these copycat Orthostats?... Some sort of Victorian Lego? And, how about the small matter that a replica would need to be eight feet tall and magnetic, then?"

"We'll be using reinforced horse manure," said Harry. "Some people build entire houses that way, so it's not rocket science. Granted, there is a tricky part. That'll be creating the iron content for the magnetism bit."

"Oh, I suppose you'll be feeding the animals with iron-filings first then, will you? And why not throw a few horseshoes over your shoulder, into the heap for good luck, too. Crikey Harry, we could just sprinkle some fairy dust along the Corridor of Light. That'd work, wouldn't it?"

"Don't worry. I've already thought about the magnetic side of things and we're covered, trust me," said Harry, eyeing Grandpa Bert, who nodded his head enthusiastically in support.

"That sounds fantastic, Harry. I'm up for any chance to see Gladys before I die. Tell me what I can do to help." Harry pointed across the yard.

"We need horses and carts for transport. Can you arrange several for first thing in the morning?"

Grandpa Bert agreed, while Lou scowled in irritation. She had no choice other than going along with her brother's idea which made her feel doubly frustrated. Not only was his plan stupid but, for once, she was desperate for it to NOT end in disaster, a disposition she did not like one bit.

Finally, with everyone thoroughly exhausted after the brainstorming session, they all turned in.

The following day, Harry was up early. He had recruited several stable hands to help before Lou and Bert arrived on the scene.

"Grab yourselves a fork and help loading the carts; we need to fill about six, altogether," suggested Harry. Bert got stuck in straight away, while Lou grudgingly picked up a fork, not wishing to appear lazy. Before long, the first two carts had been dispatched for delivery to the Orthostats by two stable hands. Afterwards, Harry led Lou and Bert to the breakfast room.

"We're gonna need all of our energy to build both replica Orthostats by hand," he said as they ferociously consumed full breakfasts.

When four more carts were loaded, they set off along the lane, Grandpa Bert riding on top of one at the front. Lou was staring like a zombie into the distance until, suddenly, she flew into a panic and jumped up. Smoke could be seen coiling up from the wooded area around the Orthostats, but realising the columns were only steam from the manure, she calmed down they arrived on site, emptying the carts, wearily.
"That's phase one complete. Now, for phase two," voiced Harry. For that, we must visit Wilfred and Lauretta; I've a favour to ask."

At the farm cottage a little later, a warm greeting awaited them all and Grandpa indulged in a lengthy catch up with his two old friends. Harry stood by patiently until eventually taking his chance to ask the favour. "May we borrow eight steel rails and a sledgehammer?" Wilf glinted back at Harry, but knew better than to ask what they were for, and replied positively.

"Take as many as ye be needing, Harry. They be stacked by the pit. We replace warped rails in the train track every summer whenever the heat twists 'em."

"Thanks Wilf. Eight is plenty," said Harry, "One for each corner."

With their business concluded, Wilf turned to Bert, singing the praises of Lou. "Your grandson, here, do proper know how to ride a horse. And he be a fearless jumper, that boy, too."

Bert winked at Lou then disclosed her most recent triumph, also advising Wilf to have a few bob on Brightlight at the next race meeting.

"I'll send Joey back with the sledgehammer and rails in a few days. The rest of us are going away for a while," shouted Bert as the cart moved off, leaving Wilfred and Lauretta waving cheerfully up the lane.

While riding directly to the stone cluster, Lou drilled Harry for more information about the next part of his plan.

"It's simple. We magnetise the steel rails first, then skewer them into the ground at each corner of the replicas," he replied. "The effect should mimic the magnetic force of the missing stone, quite well."

"Magnetise 'em? Magnetise 'em with what, though? Don't forget, we're stuck in the middle of Victorian nowhere. There is no electricity, durghh?"

"There was no electricity in neolithic times, either..." said Harry, mysteriously. "But the original ironstones are magnetic."

After offloading the first length of steel, he leaned it against an Orthostat, then passed the sledgehammer to Lou before revealing the answer she'd been waiting for.

"The original stones were simply magnetised by lightning strike."

Lou frowned.

"Oh, so, for your next trick you're going to conjure up a bolt of lightning AND direct it at the replicas, then? Thor, are we?" Lou's sarcasm bit deeply but Harry showed no reaction. Instead he began relating the history of the compass by way of explanation.

"Did you know? Small samples of naturally magnetised rock were used to make the world's first-ever compass. The word lodestone actually comes from an old word meaning leading stone.

All of the magnetised Orthostats were extracted from a band of lightning struck ironstone, close to the earth's surface. They were then chiselled into shape and transported to the site. The magnetism explains the strange hum we heard near the stones, even when the portal is inactive. Now, pass me your , I'll demonstrate.

Lou reached reluctantly into her pocket, pulled out the knife and unfolded it. But, rather than handing it to Harry, she moved the steel blade slowly towards an Orthostat. All of a sudden, the knife flew from her hand and locked onto the stone face, leaving Lou astounded. She yanked the knife away from the rock and repeated the process with the other lodestones. All of them offered the same result, and Harry smiled, then addressed her again.

"Okay. Now touch your knife blade on one of the steel rails."

Lou screwed up her face, quizzically, and walked silently over to stroke the knife blade against a length of train track, where it stuck firmly, hanging in mid-air from the rail.

"The tracks were magnetised already?" she suggested, indignantly, testing another rail with the knife.

"No, It's your knife that's magnetised. When you rubbed it against the ironstones, magnetism was transferred to the blade. On the same basis, if we brush our rails against the lodestones, they'll become charged, too." Lou was overcome with the look of a person suddenly seeing the light and Bert, who had been listening quietly, congratulated Harry.

"Clever, Harry, very clever. I think you're onto something with that idea. We could be on the way to building a pair of pretty good replicas." Lou grinned a grin which displayed both mild irritation and excitement, then grabbed the pitchforks, passing one each to Bert and Harry.

"Well, what are we waiting for? Let's get building. I'm a convert."

"Okay, but we'll magnetise the rails first, then hammer them into the ground to make roughly square frames which we can fill with manure."

Over the next few minutes, the three of them joined forces, struggling to draw the massive steel rails back and forth against the lodestones like giant violin bows. Eventually, all eight were charged, and after knocking them into the ground by standing on the cart, a soggy mixture of horse faeces, straw and urine was added. As the heaps grew steadily taller, the ragged outline was smoothed by Lou with her bare hands until, finally, they all stood back proudly to admire their workmanship.

"Ummm... Smelltastic," chortled Lou, sniffing her fingers. "Let's get back to the stables for a wash.

I reek something chronic. "

Reconvening in Bert's room after a stable-yard hose down and a lengthy bath, all three scoffed a hearty meal prepared by Joey. At the same time, Lou questioned Harry, enthusiastically. "So, which one of us gets to ride which horse through the portal? Cuz I bagsy Brightlight." Harry took a swig of tea, then answered.

"You and I will ride, two-up, on Brightlight and Grandpa can take Longshadow. We'll bring both horses back another day, along with a spark plug to fix the trail bike. We can demolish the replicas once the bike is fixed and the horses are home. It's probably better that no one else rides an animal along the Corridor of Light, accidentally finding themselves in another time dimension."

With everyone agreed, they turned in, but lying in bed, Harry could not sleep. He was feeling the enormous responsibility resting on his shoulders. What if his inventive repair job failed? After thirty-six years, this was the only hope for Bert and Gladys to be reunited. Furthermore, without a return to 1979, how could he help wipe out the Deathmongers in 2079. Being stuck, might sound the death knell for Juno and Stella. Three generations of his family were in jeopardy and Harry was starting to wish he'd left the Corridor of Light well alone in the first place.

The next morning, an unusually excited Brightlight was led from the stable at 4am. It was as though the horse knew something was afoot. Amid the swirling mist, Harry strapped a saddle to the horse's back, then repeated the process with Longshadow. Joey arrived, along with the yard staff, and after wishing them all a second fond farewell, Harry, Lou and Bert set off up the lane, their minds filled with apprehension. At the copse, both horses circled the cluster of eight Orthostats while their riders checked everything was in order. The two fake stones looked a perfect match, apart from gentle columns of steam which rose into the air above each one.

Waiting impatiently for sunrise, they listened to the sound of bleating sheep and breathed in air, tainted by pungent horse manure. The distinct taste of bitter magnetism was seasoned with a twist of heavy grass pollen, which drifted across the glade in the occasional breeze.

Finally, they took up position at the eastern end of the cluster, and as the sun rose, no one dared speak. Their minds were consumed by a common thought. Would... Could.... Harry's portal-boost idea work? If not, the stable yard beckoned once more. They would all be trapped in 1879 for life.

A faint hum was audible above the chirping birds as lengthy shadows began forming on either side of the corridor, and a central shaft of strong sunlight signalled the moment to set off. Lou turned to smile briefly at Grandpa Bert, then cantered into the Corridor of Light with Harry clinging to her waist. Brightlight, quickly built up speed and was closely followed by Longshadow until both horses reached a gallop, their manes flowing backwards in the wind like ribbons. Bert's bushy eyebrows rippled as Lou tapped Brightlight's neck three times to initiate a final burst of speed. Passing the steaming replicas with both horses flat out, a series of lightning bolts signalled their safe passage through the portal, after which an eerie calm descended.

They pulled up and looked back to find the steaming manure piles gone and a significant gap in the wooden fence confirmed that all three family members were home. Grandpa Bert gazed across his own land for the first time in thirty-six years.

"I'm starting to love that manky bale-stack," laughed Lou in Harry's direction, as their grandfather sat motionless astride Longshadow, trembling slightly.

"At last. My whole family are home, together!" said Harry under his breath, before turning to Grandpa Bert. "Grandma Gladys lives in a cottage over there." He pointed across the fields, and Bert nodded without speaking. He patted his grandson's shoulder, then flicking Longshadow's reins and set off at a trot.

Harry and Lou followed slowly until Bert suddenly broke into a gallop, finally dismounting at the cottage and slinking up the garden path. The front door opened instantly and a familiar voice rang out.

"Bert Scrambles, if you're expecting breakfast, you'd better get round to the hen house and fetch a couple of large eggs, pronto. Then we'll see."

Smiling at her grandchildren over the hedge, Grandma Gladys shouted out. "Well, Harry. You certainly did surprise me this time." With a wave, she disappeared back inside the house, while Harry took Longshadow by the reigns and they all trotted off.

CHAPTER 11.
DEATHMONGER
DEATH?

Several days later, both horses were back in 1879 and the repaired trail bike had been returned to 1979. Harry and Lou had also built up sufficient energy to consider their next task. They agreed that enough fairy flies should now have been gathered in 2079, and were desperate to deal the monstrous Deathmonger wasps a final deadly blow.

Preparing to enter the Corridor of Light, Harry clutched Dirtbag in one hand, climbed onto the back of the trail bike and wrapped his spare arm around Lou's waist. After a cursory backward glance, she accelerated through the portal, and seconds later, with a flash, they arrived in the year 2079.

Thirteen days had transpired since the Deathmonger eradication sanction issued by Dr Shizzle. Thousands of fairy wasps were now safely stored in test tubes of nutrient liquid, ready for the final task; the transfer of the fairy vials into the water tanks below each wasp housing. This would initiate the process of invading the nests and the subsequent laying of fairy fly eggs among the Deathmonger Larvae. What could possibly go wrong?

Arriving at Juno's, Harry hopped off the motorbike, lowered Dirtbag to the floor and stepped over the box hedge into her pretty garden. Juno ran across the lawn, barely noticed by Harry whose gaze had been drawn to the enormous battery tower behind the house. As the crane hoisted yet another concrete block majestically into place, he noticed two dark shadows launching from a gap between the blocks and flying off into the nearby trees. Before Harry could study the scene further, Juno called out, smiling broadly.

"So, here we are. The day of reckoning for those monstrous Deathmongers," she affirmed.
"Let's hope so," replied Harry in an apprehensive tone. "Have we collected enough fairy wasps?"

"Yes, Mum's gathered stock from all over the world. She and Shizzle are checking the final packages in the house as we speak. We'll soon be ready to deliver the fairy flies to the buffer zone for distribution by robot among the Deathmonger nests. All Warnet housings have been colour coded green, so as not to be targeted. They'll be essential to keep the compound free from pests while the Deathmongers die out." Harry nodded, then

Stella and Doctor Shizzle arrived in the garden with a tray of tea and cakes. Partaking of the scrumptious picnic food, they listened as Gideon Shizzle declared the Deathmonger eradication plan ready to execute, praising Harry for his water tanker idea. It seemed the Deathmongers had successfully been kept inside the compound for the past weeks with no further sign of escape.

"The up and coming infestation of nests will reduce the Deathmonger population to zero in an ecologically sound manner with no harm to society in general," stated Shizzle. "Furthermore, the whole Deathmonger escape thing has been kept a secret to avoid unnecessary public panic," he added, bombastically.

Harry and Lou eyed one another uncomfortably. Brushing the truth of the matter under the carpet did not seem like a good idea to either of them.

With everyone falling silent, Juno placed a half scone onto the floor for Dirtbag, who began licking off the cream until suddenly, the cat's ears pricked up. With hackles rising quickly along the spiny ridge of his arched back, Dirtbag sprang across the grass and disappeared into the undergrowth, leaving everyone chuckling loudly.

"Your cat is so feral. It prefers natural prey to easy pickings," laughed Juno as a high pitched yowl accompanied the violent shaking of nearby bushes. A long, unexpected stillness followed, and Harry suddenly looked nervous.

He glared uneasily after the feral cat for several seconds, then jumped to his feet, sprinted across the garden, and parted the bushes. Dirtbag lay motionless on the floor, with a monstrous Deathmonger wasp plucking away at a patch of fur. The cat's wild eyes displayed a mixture of fear and anger, and without thinking, Harry grabbed a stick from the ground, then lunged at the wasp. The Deathmonger's twitching antennae immediately sensed the attack and it lifted effortlessly into the air, flashing its tiger-striped abdomen and dagger-like sting. As the fearsome insect flew directly at Harry, he swung the stick furiously, but the wasp swerved, avoiding the weapon and circled for a further attack. A split second later, two jagged mandibles gripped Harry's T-shirt sleeve and his bare arm was tickled by a set of lacy wings. A sharp, painful stinging sensation spread through Harry's upper arm, and expecting total paralysis, he closed his eyes in resignation as the numbness quickly set in. Imagining the raw venom pumping around his veins, he pictured the killer wasp, sucking his blood while conscious, but frozen and unable to respond. Harry prayed for a quick death, and re-opened his eyes, struggling to focus. For some reason, the expected fateful progression had failed to occur, and clearing his vision with a series of quick blinks, he spotted the monstrous Deathmonger's evil compound eyes staring up from the floor, where it lay, stone dead. Turning slowly, Harry's gaze met with Juno's, her eyes displaying a hollow glare, with no sign of the usual bright sparkle.

Sorry Harry, sorry wasp, but I had to do it. I had to crush that beast against your arm," she cried, dropping the stick. Her apologetic voice rang loud in Harry's ear, but only for a second as, tilting his head, he registered another sound. The faint, yet unnerving hum of a distant swarm came from behind the house, and rose rapidly in volume as Harry shouted a disjointed warning.

"A nest in the battery tower... Pheromone release...... More wasps on the way.... Get in the house, quick."

Scooping up Dirtbag, he surged towards the patio doors as the angry cloud of killer wasps rolled in from the high tower. The Deathmongers were closing fast, and Stella reached the house first, followed by Shizzle, who pulled Lou roughly inside. Juno and Harry were some yards behind, twisting their heads in terror to focus on the buzzing dark swarm as they ran. Seconds later, both of them dived through the doors and Harry launched Dirtbag onto the sofa, before dropping to the lounge floor on top of Juno. Stella slammed the patio doors shut and a dozen Kamikaze Deathmongers bounced hard against the glass. The huge wasps dropped dead to the ground, killed on impact but releasing a pheromone smog, which sent the angry swarm into a heightened frenzy.

Thousands of Deathmongers buzzed, bounced and billowed around the doors and windows, searching for a way in, and the dense cloud plunged the entire house into a fearful darkness. Suddenly, however, the Deathmonger fog cleared as the giant insects swirled away. They were gone into the sky, but for how long?

Harry, though pale and breathless, picked himself up and turned quickly to Stella. "Fetch me the anti-venom for Dirtbag, fast. Everyone else, check all the doors and windows." He dropped onto the sofa, lifted Dirtbag gently onto his knee and stroked the cat's venom-locked body.

"We'll soon have you sorted out, Dirtbag," said Harry, reassuringly as Stella returned swiftly and administered the injection. A moment later, Lou, Juno, and Shizzle arrived, confirming that all windows and doors were secure, and Harry breathed out heavily then began chewing his bottom lip. With a dry, tight throat, he addressed Juno in a hoarse voice. "Thanks for helping me, back there. That slap was just what I needed." Juno smiled weakly.

"I'm sorry for being so vicious with my stick on your arm, but the wasp had to die in one blow. It would have killed you, otherwise."

Collapsing into empty chairs around the room, a strange feeling of euphoria washed over them all. It was hard to believe that somehow they had survived the crazed insect attack, and the relief escalated when Dirtbag rose to his feet on Harry's lap, arched his back in a major stretch and yawned a lengthy yawn. Juno reached over to offer comfort, but suddenly, the feral beast hopped down and scuttled over to the fireplace, meowing loudly. A small black cloud poofed out into the room, followed by another, much larger soot ball.

"The wasps. They are in the chimney!" belched Harry, jumping to his feet and grabbing a cushion from the settee.

"Sorry, Stella!" He darted to the kitchen and drenched the cushion under the tap, then returned, jamming it violently up the chimney. A cloud of acrid black dust cascaded into the room, covering Harry's face, but with the vent successfully blocked, he dropped to his knees in front of the others.

"The wet soot'll give those Deathmonger goons a nasty cough if they try chewing through the cushion," he said, pulling himself up with the help of a coffee table, before slumping onto what remained of the sofa.

A jaded, almost sleepy feeling had come over each and every one of them as they contemplated the fact that someone, somehow, still had to deliver the fairy wasps to the buffer zone. Failure to carry out this simple task would leave the entire planet doomed. They were surrounded by a bunch of riled predators, each armed with lethal stings and night vision, whilst the outside world was oblivious to their plight, and anyway, the rest of humanity was devoid of weapons, powerless to help... Nothing could now prevent the Deathmongers from colonising the world. A process, already underway.

Shizzle was a broken man, his utopian dream in tatters. For the first time he accepted the full force of responsibility. He had nurtured the deadly giant insects and felt utterly ashamed. As Harry studied the Doctor's forlorn posture, he attempted to string together a few words of optimism.

"Don't worry, Doctor Shizzle, we're not finished yet. The fairy flies are in here with us. We just need to figure out how to neutralise the Deathmonger wasps in the crane tower, so we can get the fairy vials to the buffer zone. That can't be too hard, can it?"

"Can't be hard, can't be hard?" repeated Lou. "Ten thousand, air born killing machines, whose best buddies we've just murdered, are circling the house, hell-bent on revenge? We can't just tip-toe past their nest carrying fragile test tubes filled with defenceless fairy flies. The task sure sounds hard to me, and let's not forget. MUM'LL KILL US IF WE GET KILLED."

After studying Harry's face for signs of optimism, Juno gripped him by the arm. "If anyone CAN come up with a plan to get us out of this mess, you are that person, Harry... It's just a case of thinking outside the box, like you did to solve the cryptic clue..."

Her voice was interrupted by a faint clicking sound at the back of the house and she spun nervously towards the noise, while Harry leapt from his seat and edged closer. Placing the palm of one hand against a wooden wall panel, he was shocked to feel a faint, scratchy vibration.

"Stella, is your house built on a concrete pad?" he demanded.

"No, I don't think so. It was a timber shell, erected on bare earth," she replied in a shocked voice. We only intended to live here for a few months, but liked it so much we decided to stay. Why?"

"The wasps are burrowing under the walls. We're about to be in serious trouble of the big and very stingy variety." Harry's attempt at humour fell on deaf ears as a veil of fear spread across the room and the echo of additional clicking noises spread rapidly. The Deathmongers were coming.

"Fetch water, fast," yelled Harry. "We need a chain of bowls and buckets filling from the sink, to soak the base of the walls and clag their mandibles." He began peeling back the vinyl floor covering and within seconds, Lou had delivered the first full bowl of water, while Stella threw several more empty buckets from the utility room which were frantically put to work. The soil at the foot of three external walls was soon wetted, but as they rushed to the fourth, a patch of floor rose ominously in front of them like a molehill. Two wriggling antennae appeared through the dirt, and in a gut reaction, Harry hurled an entire bucket of water at the wasp's head. The insect's antennae disappeared back into the soil, and Lou jammed her heel down the hole, cramming wet earth into the void. They continued the dousing in silent fear until gradually the clicking sounds faded away and everyone relaxed.

"Thank heavens wasp mandibles make a noise when they dig," spluttered Lou, collapsing onto the cushion-less sofa with her brother. Harry peered around the room at four pasty faces, and Stella, who had also noticed the drained expressions, went off to make tea and sandwiches in an attempt to bolster the group. Twenty minutes later, a hungry munching signalled the return of a semblance of normality. Nevertheless, inside, Harry felt weak. He was still craving sugar, despite consuming most of the biscuits on offer, and reaching into his trouser pocket, he pulled out the congealed sherbet pips and offered them around. Even Doctor Shizzle consumed a welded chunk of the boiled sweets in the manner of a small schoolboy, meaning Harry's supply rapidly disappeared. Recognising the serious nature of the dilemma, Lou rummaged through her own jacket and contributed an additional handful of individually wrapped items.

"Black Jacks and Fruit Salad," she offered, "Help yourselves." Eventually, all of the goffs were guzzled and Harry stood up.

"I've had an idea. This might not work, but it's our only hope." For once, Lou showed no sign of argument as Harry directed his gaze at Stella. "That stack of radio masts I saw in your utility room, could they be used to form a sound barrier around the nest in the battery tower? And can we activate the fence from inside the house?"

"Yes, we keep spare masts to replace those around the main compound. Occasionally, during storms, they suffer lightning damage, and we need to fit new ones before the Deathmongers emerge from their nests afterwards."

Half an hour later, Harry brandished a home made longbow he had constructed by lashing three wispy antennae together to create good tension. After stretching and tying off the taut bowstring, he moved over to a window at the back of the house. The battery stack was about twenty yards away and Harry revealed further details of his plan. He intended to fire four antennae into the ground, creating a miniature compound around the rogue nest. A vile of fairy flies would then need to be delivered near to the nest before any roaming Deathmongers were, somehow, coaxed back to protect their brood. Finally, once all of the wasps were inside, the fence could be activated. Harry's scheme was dangerous, but by isolating the rogue

Deathmongers, fairy fly wasps could infest the nest in the battery stack and it would be safe to deliver the rest of the viles to the compound."

A look of alarm spread around the room as details of the risky plan sank in, but, with Lou designated window monitor, Harry had soon fired the first antennae tentatively from the bow. After a couple of misses, four posts were successfully speared into position, and Lou slammed the window shut, turning with a sullen look on her face.

"So far so good, Harry, but someone's gonna have to go outside. You can't fire the fairy flies from a bow. And just so's you know it; that someone ain't gonna be me." Lou cast her eyes beadily around the room, and unexpectedly, Dr Shizzle stepped forward.

"It was me who created the Deathmonger species, so I should be the one taking the risk now. I'll plant the fairy fly wasps then make a noise near the nest. The Deathmonger scouts will send a pheromone attack message, and once the workers return, someone can switch on the sound barrier and I'll duck back through it. Any risk of getting stung will only last for a couple of minutes. Everything should be fine, and we do have anti-venom."

The room went quiet for several seconds, then Harry nodded and began organising the others around the task.

"Lou. I want you to be crane operator. We need to be able to move a block up and down, as well as in towards the tower, and out. Is there a manual override for the crane's operation inside the house?" he threw a questioning glance at Stella, who responded quickly.

"Yes, in my office."

"Good. So, I suggest Doctor Shizzle climbs onto a concrete block, then keeps completely still while Lou raises him to the nest. The wasps are used to the constant up and down movement of the blocks and should not be alarmed at all. This will buy time for you to go unnoticed, Dr Shizzle, while preparing to deliver the fairy flies successfully."

Shizzle nodded back at Harry.

"Good idea, Harry. Afterwards, I'll make sure that I'm seen. The workers will rush back to the nest, Lou can switch on and then manoeuvre me back through the high-frequency fence to safety. I will wear a protective suit, and any wasps clinging to it will be knocked back into the compound by the sound waves. I only need a suit strong enough to survive Deathmonger attack for a few seconds."

Harry and Lou looked solemnly at one another, knowing that what Shizzle had just described was a probable suicide mission. Still, someone had to do it.

"I have two bee suits in my utility room," Offered Stella, "You could wear one inside another. The

Deathmongers wouldn't have time to cut through both suits, surely?"

"Yes, twin suits might do the trick," replied Shizzle, "But if I do get stung, make sure we have plenty of anti-venom ready." Stella nodded, and Harry bowed his head quietly. The bee suits were tough cotton, but their flimsy veils didn't sound so good. He recalled how easily a single Deathmonger had carved through the butterfly net a few days earlier. After racking his brains, he suddenly blurted out an idea.

"This may sound crazy, but if we empty Juno's goldfish bowl, you could wear it like a helmet, Dr Shizzle. The Deathmongers wouldn't be able to attack your face through that." He pointed to a large, round, glass bowl, sitting on a shelf in the corner.

"Your fish'll be fine in a bucket for half an hour," added Harry, smiling at Juno.

And so it was decided. Shizzle, was dressed in a doubled-up bee suit, worn over his own clothes and donned the unlikely glass helmet, stuffed tightly with wet rags around his shoulders to form a seal. Afterwards, Stella handed over a small plastic vessel containing the nutrient water and a double dose of fairy flies. Shizzle attached these carefully by a carrying handle to the belt around his waist and finally, Harry stepped up with what looked like several long wooden lollypop sticks.

"Keep these safe, Doctor Shizzle. They need to be placed into the water vessel outside the nest. Fairy flies are too small to break the surface tension of water by themselves; they must crawl up the sticks to have a chance of reaching the Deathmonger's nest. Good luck, and thanks for doing this."

Shizzle placed one hand momentarily on Stella's shoulder and then stepped out through the patio doors, sliding them gently closed behind him.

Once outside, the Doctor gave a distorted smile through the glass of the goldfish bowl and edged slowly around the house. Approaching the crane, he scoured the air for Deathmongers, before climbing onto a concrete block at ground level. He clung nervously to the chain, which was attached by a hook to a loop in the concrete, and waited for Lou to lift him into the air. A second later, she eased back on the lever and the slab moved gently upwards.

Within two more minutes, Shizzle was three feet below the nest, where a steady stream of Deathmonger wasps could be seen flying in and out of the dark entrance, which was patrolled by wasp scouts. The previously stacked blocks were protecting the steel latticework of the central, vertical crane body which housed a huge papery nest, visible only through gaps in the construction. Lou paused the ascent and began moving Shizzle horizontally. As he approached a ledge beneath the nest, the Doctor leaned out from his concrete plinth, gripping the chain tightly with one hand and unclipped the water bowl from his waist. Then he let go of the chain to tentatively remove the lid. Wobbling on the block, Shizzle looked nervously at the hard ground twenty-five feet below. He steadied himself just as two scout wasps began to check him out, but the Doctor remained perfectly calm, while reaching slowly over to the crane tower and sliding the vessel gingerly into place. After moving back quickly, he suddenly remembered the wooden lollipop sticks.

The repeated movements had, by now, set the Deathmonger scouts on high alert and this provoked immediate action as pheromone signals were released, spreading quickly among the nearby wasps. Worker wasps rushed urgently from all around to defend the nest, while Harry, Lou, Stella and Juno peered helplessly through the window. All too soon, thousands of aggressive Deathmongers were homing in on Shizzle.

A look of intense fear spread across the Doctor's face as the collective buzz of the approaching swarm of killer wasps became so loud that it penetrated the walls of the little wooden house, making the windows rattle. Then, the first of the Deathmongers began their attack.

At the controls of the crane, Lou swung the concrete block frantically away from the nest, right through the angry cloud, watching as hundreds of wasps bounced off the fishbowl.

With more and more Deathmongers skidding against the glass, fury rose among the swarm. The frustrated wasps were unable to empty their venom-filled pump guns with no access to Shizzle because they had nothing to cling onto. It seemed the glass bowl was doing a brilliant job.

Harry, Juno and Stella let out tense cheers, and Lou concentrated on moving the block towards the high-frequency barrier. "Prepare to switch on the fence," she bawled. "Nearly all the wasps are inside the compound."

With dozens of monstrous Deathmongers pummelling Doctor Shizzle, his face disappeared, the predatory insects bouncing furiously back and forth against the impenetrable glass bowl. The wasp's efforts to target Shizzle's head proved futile until, suddenly, a few Deathmongers moved down his body, quickly gaining purchase on the fabric of the bee suit. Within seconds, they had carved open the first layer like a knife through butter. Several wasps moved inside the suit, and Stella glanced frantically at Harry, who was repeatedly jabbing the start button of the high-frequency fence.

The barrier hummed into life and Stella breathed a sigh of relief. "Now, get him out of there," she shrieked at Lou. Shizzle's face gradually reappeared as hundreds of wasps were swept back towards the nest by the radio waves between the masts, but the look of intense fear had not left him. Several Deathmongers were moving inside the first bee suit. They were protected and unable to be knocked clear by the sound barrier. These wasps were already cutting deep into the second layer of fabric. Dr Shizzle snatched frantically at a squirming Deathmonger, pulling it out through the torn outer suit and crushing it with his gloved hand, but he could not work fast enough. Three more wasps having lacerated the second suit, moved beyond and an expression of agony grew on Shizzle's face as multiple stings penetrated his clothing. The Doctor dropped purposely forwards against the concrete block in an attempt to crush the last few wasps and let out lengthy muffled screams from inside the glass jar as venom surged into his bloodstream. His head slumped against the concrete, shattering the fishbowl.

Harry and the others, watched as Doctor Shizzle's pale, motionless face turned steadily greyer, while the crushed killer wasps continued to pump poison, even after their death. Lou's hands shook at the controls as the crane reached ground level, and Stella dashed outside, armed with the anti-venom syringes, closely followed by Harry.

Approaching the broken glass of the goldfish bowl, she stooped to inject Shizzle directly in the neck, then, after hovering over him for a few seconds, she shooed Harry away, forlornly.

"It's no good," she muttered. "Doctor Shizzle's heart was paralysed by the poison. The anti-venom came too late." Stella sounded calm as she stepped away from the body, but had to gather herself privately. By the time the others arrived on the scene, she felt ready to talk again.

"Doctor Shizzle was the bravest of men. He achieved what he set out to do, and as a result, the first step of Harry's plan is a success. Shizzle knew the risks. Now it's up to us to destroy the entire deadly Deathmonger species in his memory."

The group stood in silent salute of Shizzle's sacrifice for several minutes before filing quietly back to the house. The task of distributing the minuscule parasitoids to the Deathmonger nests inside the main compound could safely begin.

Two days later, the last batch of fairy flies had been added to the last water tank beneath the final Deathmonger nest. Afterwards, the field robots were re-programmed to resume their usual duties. The miniscule pregnant fairy flies soon clambered out of the water and moved unseen, up the wooden sticks. They scaled the tank support wires to access the nests through ventilation slats in the wasp housings. Fairy wasp eggs hatched in their millions, devouring the Deathmonger larvae to slaughter the next generation of killer wasps in full accordance with nature's rules.

The demise of the monstrous Deathmonger breed would serve as a valuable lesson to mankind. It showed how easily things can turn from good to bad, from utopia to dystopia.

Maybe one day, the ongoing quest for a genuinely perfect utopian world would find success, and for now, disaster had been averted.

On the day of the sibling's departure, Harry faced one more unpleasant task. His delivery of a final goodbye to Juno. After their recent adventures, a close connection had formed with this girl, Harry's great great granddaughter, but this was one fact he could never reveal.

The two of them sat in the garden enduring an awkward silence for several minutes, each picking their fingers nervously. Eventually, Harry stood and thrust one hand deep into his trouser pocket. He pulled out his St Christopher's medal in two pieces and held up half of the medallion with a weak smile, the chain still attached. Juno hung it around her neck, while Harry dropped the other piece into the palm of his hand. "I borrowed your mother's tin snips to do the damage. When I get home, I'll solder a new ring onto my half and fit a new chain. St Christopher is the Patron Saint of travel, you know. He'll look after both of us whenever we're apart."

"Thank you," replied Juno, "But I'll be expecting you to call in for regular cups of tea from now on."

Harry smiled. "I'll be back whenever I can be... Count on it." With that, he winked and walked away.

Once the siblings had left for home, life got back to normal for Juno, but several weeks later, she sat in the garden, recalling her recent adventures.

Twiddling the St Christopher between finger and thumb, the unusual gift stoked a strange feeling of familiarity and a cog suddenly turned inside her head. With her heart beating wildly in her chest, she rushed to the bedroom and threw open the wooden trinket box on top of the dressing table. Juno was searching for an item seen only once before. She removed the photos and passports of her great grandmother, tossing these aside irritably as her slender fingers shuffled around in the box. Suddenly, losing her patience, she upended the entire thing, sending further contents tumbling across the dresser. Juno's eyes immediately latched onto a tarnished silver chain with a jagged, half-moon pendant on a loop at one end. Lifting it, she stroked the uneven edge for several seconds, then offered it tentatively against the half of a St Christopher, worn around her own neck. Juno's eyes glazed over as she stared into the mirror. The two halves fitted perfectly and she collapsed onto the bed.

The siblings were in strange moods on the day of their departure from the year 2079. Recent events had left them both mentally and physically drained. They were splayed out flat on their backs in the evening sunlight, waiting for the Corridor of Light, until, finally, racing down the bank to mount the trail bike.

As they zoomed between the Orthostats, their hair ruffled in the wind, then, in a flash, Harry and Lou were back where it had all begun.

A few weeks later, Lou's two best friends arrived to stay once more. It was half term. Harry stood nearby, tinkering with his car and feeling nervous as he earwigged the conversation between Rose and Lou. Eventually, he wandered over, tapping a spanner against the palm of his hand. "You've been to Turkey, I hear?" he said.

"Yes. On a school trip, and it was ace. Have you been anywhere like that before?"

"No... Never abroad. I think time travel would be more my cup of tea," he chuckled.

"Oh yes. To visit another time dimension, how exciting that would be," If only it were possible." She laughed, then pointed to the chain around Harry's neck.

"Your St Christopher looks a bit battered. I'd get that fixed first, if I were you."

Harry smiled and wandered back to the car. Sitting inside Rivet, he slid his hands back and forth around the steering wheel. There was no denying it. Rose was a very nice girl, simple as that. There was nothing to be afraid of. She would soon be a part of his family and he realised that while worrying about becoming a proper part of one family, he had become a part of two. One in the present and another in the future. Life was good.

Just then, a wasp dropped through the sunroof.

Harry watched the Tiger-Striped Goon bounce across the windscreen and then it turned to hover right in front of him.

Staring back at the two shining compound and three simple eyes in between, he did not flinch, and a second later the wasp exited through the side window.

Harry's mind flashed back to the Deathmongers of 2079 and the world's smallest insects, the fairy flies; a tiny wasp that had saved the utopian world.

"Sometimes you just have to love wasps... But only sometimes," he said out loud.

THE END

EPILOGUE.

With the sun low in the sky, the air in the grassy glade was warm as the distant sound of a tractor engine faded to leave a middle-aged man standing alone. Stooping down to gather a single stem of meadow grass, his flat cap fell to the floor, and picking it up with one hand, he swiped it against his knee, sending out a cloud of dust. The minute particles danced through beams of evening sunlight before vanishing into the long shadows cast on either side of the light source.

The man stood up, the hunching of his strong shoulders, caused by years of lifting heavy corn sacks, obvious. He rolled the grass stem between finger and thumb, then bit the end to release a sweet juice inside his mouth. The flavour reminded him of nettle tea, given to him as a boy, and a feeling of comfort came over him. Breathing deeply through his nose, the scent of bluebells filled both nostrils, and he made a mental note to transplant the flower bulbs. Gladys will not want those beautiful wild flowers buried by the foundations of an air-raid shelter, he thought, setting off up the lane towards his beloved potato field.

To the man's left, barley awns swished and swayed in the breeze, and snapping off a single ear, he counted the individual grains. Twenty four, twenty-five, twenty-six. Good. The frequent rains had kept his crops well watered this year. Perfect conditions for the shallow limestone soil of the heath.

Arriving at the potato field, the man dropped on one knee and plunged a strong hand deep into the earth. His fingers groped around in the loose soil, gripping a small potato, which he withdrew to examine carefully. Only four weeks to harvest and no sign of scab. Just what he'd been hoping for. The man walked back to the glade, stopping at its eastern edge to remove his grubby jacket which he hung on the branch of a tree. Then, turning with a renewed sense of urgency, he made a beeline towards the garden spade, which was leaning against a rock, one hundred yards away. May as well get on and dig those bluebells up while I'm waiting for John, he mused, striding towards the implement. Suddenly, a shimmering light enveloped him, and everything went hazy. Startled, the man raised his hands in front of his eyes and blinked long and hard. As a blast of chilled air hit his face, he was left with an inexplicable sense of fear, and noticed that the spade was gone.

Feeling cold, he set off to fetch his jacket, the sweat patches under both armpits feeling like ice against his bare skin. As goosebumps travelled rapidly down both arms, the man reached the eastern edge of the glade and halted abruptly, letting the grass stem dropped from his mouth.

His head twitched erratically as both eyes scoured the area to his left and right in desperation. The plain fact was that the tree upon which he had hung his coat was gone, and his jacket was also missing. A deep sense of panic was intensified as he realised that the sweet fragrance of bluebells had also been replaced; by the strong smell of animal manure. Looking around, he saw a flock of sheep in an adjacent field and the man gripped his cap between finger and thumb, hutching it back over his head as he scratched the nape of his neck. In slow motion, he turned towards his beloved potato field... A throng of birds could be seen chasing a plough, pulled by two large horses across bare earth, and the man opened his fist slowly, gazing at the small white potato in astonishment.

ROB SCARBOROUGH

The Deathmonger Wasp

ACKNOWLEDGEMENT

Thanks go to Dad, a true inventor,
and to our family farm, the
setting for these stories.
Also, thankyou Ann Kilroy, for the
glorious watercolour illustrations.

An especially big round of applause to wasps,
large and small, scary and annoying. All of
them being a crucial part of the ecosystem.
Please love and respect them as such.

A young inventor and his trickster, elder sister embark on vile, smelly and time travelling 1970s on-farm capers.

Daft Harry And The Tiger Striped Goons. Book 1

Harry and Lou's first battle with wasps and jewel thieves.

Daft Harry And The Mystery Of The Ginger Cake Fake... Book 2

Could the fake robbery of the Imperial State Crown have actually happened? Harry and Lou investigate.

The Corridor Of Light. Book 3

Harry and Lou discover a neolithic time portal.